Grammar Workshop™

TOOLS FOR WRITING

Level Orange

Beverly Ann Chin, Ph.D.

Senior Series Consultant
Professor of English
University of Montana
Missoula, MT

Sadlier School

Reviewers

The publisher wishes to thank the following teachers for their thorough review and thoughtful comments on portions of the series prior to publication.

Wendy Alessio
Our Lady of the Prairie Catholic School
Belle Plaine, MN

Tracy Camarda-Harrow
Holy Family School
New Rochelle, NY

Cathleen Cotgreave
Saint Leo the Great
Lincroft, NJ

Jennifer A. Dee
St. Philip School
Melbourne, KY

Carolyn Fay
George M. Davis Elementary School
New Rochelle, NY

Denise C. Jordan, M.A. Ed.
Next Generation Academics, Inc.
Bradenton, FL

Lisa Kelly
Mt. Bethel Christian Academy
Marietta, GA

Tadem Perok
Charleroi Elementary Center
Charleroi, PA

Jill Dee Wagner
Saint Mary's Hall
San Antonio, TX

Cover Series Design: Silver Linings Studios; **Cover Illustration:** Ian Naylor.

Photo Credits: Adobe Stock/lizziemaher: 196. age fotostock/Andre Seale: 80. Alamy Stock Photo/Bill Brooks: 113; D. Hurst: 17 *left*; Ablestock: 218; GhostWorx Images/William Baker: 198; Hero Images Inc.: 236; image100: 60. The American Library Association: 34. Animals Animals/Michael Fogden: 117. Associated Press/Pablo Martinez Monsivais: 170. Dreamstime.com/Viacheslav Iacobchuk: 172; Starper: 82. Getty Images/Tim Flach: 45; Mike Powell: 140; Bettmann: 16, 94; Disney ABC Television Group/Adam Taylor: 61; Dorling Kindersley/Steve Lyne: 89; Fuse: 184; Jupiterimages: 180; Photodisc: 70, 130; Stockbyte: 77; Stringer/AFP: 62; The Image Bank/Diehm: 8; The Image Bank/Tony Anderson: 46; The Image Bank/Gary Vestal: 24; The Image Bank/Simon Wilkinson: 112; The Image Bank/Photo & Co: 128. www.goodtimestove.com: 13. Incorporated Research Institute for Seismology/www.iris.edu: 192. iStockphoto.com/engineer89: 90; kycstudio: 17 *center*. Levi Strauss & Co. Archives: 17 *right*. Masterfile/Jeremy Woodhouse: 20. Punchstock/Digital Vision: 76, 120; Tom Brakefield: 124; Kraig Scarbinsky: 88; Heinrich van der Berg: 126; National Geographic: 169; Photodisc: 10, 48, 64, 152, 163, 194; Photographer's Choice: 209; Stockbyte: 208. Shutterstock.com/andante: 171; f11photo: 168; IAS75: 86; iofoto: 118; LaurensT: 30; mundoview: 28; otnaydur: 229; PHB.cz (Richard Semik): 31; Poznyakov: 230; Sinelev: 176; David Dea: 22; Peder Digre: 160; Johanna Goodyear: 155; David MacFarlane: 53; Christian Mueller: 40; Glenda M. Powers: 144; Stephen Rees: 216; Tina Rencelj: 177; Dario Sabljak: 217; Brian Upton: 125; Monkey Business Images: 242. SuperStock/Peter Barritt: 92; age fotostock: 81, 114, 228; Creatas: 84. Thinkstock/Fuse: 183; Jupiterimages: 182.

Illustrators: Ron Berg: 18, 32, 65, 66, 72, 73, 164,165, 167, 220, 223. Ken Bowser: 11, 42, 68, 69, 95, 132, 134, 135, 143, 212, 213, 214. John Ceballos: 49, 50, 100, 101, 102, 210. CD Hullinger: 104, 106, 148, 150, 178, 200, 201, 202. Mena Dolobowsky: 78, 145, 147. Nathan Jarvis: 12. Martin Lemelman: 96, 98, 99, 185, 186, 204, 206. Ian Naylor: i, 6, 7, 237, 243, 249, 250, 252, 253, 254, 255, 256. Zina Saunders: 26, 116, 119, 122. Sam Ward: 44. Paul Weiner: 136, 138, 139, 224, 225, 227.

CONTENTS

UNIT 5 **PRONOUNS**

UNIT 6 CAPITALIZATION, PUNCTUATION, AND SPELLING

NOTE TO STUDENTS

You already know how to read, speak, and write English. So why should you learn grammar?

What Is Grammar?

Like all languages, English has rules about how words can be put together in sentences. Learning these rules will help you to speak and write so that everyone understands you. When you study grammar, you learn that words in English can be grouped into different parts. These parts include nouns, verbs, adjectives, adverbs, and pronouns. Grammar tells you how to put these parts together correctly.

How Will Grammar Help You?

Knowing grammar will help you to become a better reader, speaker, and writer. Knowing how language works will help you to read with more understanding. It will help you to express your feelings and ideas clearly. Your writing will be easier to follow. You will also make fewer mistakes when you do homework and take tests.

What Is Grammar Workshop?

GRAMMAR WORKSHOP is designed to teach you the rules of English and to give you lots and lots of practice. This book is called a WORKSHOP because it teaches in ways that make you work. You don't just read and memorize. You have to Learn, Practice, and Write.

Ready, Set, Go Grammar!

Now it's time to get started. Have fun, learn those rules—and go grammar!

Lesson 1: **Kinds of Sentences**

LEARN

A **sentence** is a group of words that expresses a complete thought.

■ There are four kinds of sentences.

A **declarative sentence** makes a statement.
It ends with a period (.).

> We watched a movie about volcanoes.

An **interrogative sentence** asks a question.
It ends with a question mark (**?**).

> Have you ever seen a volcano?

An **imperative sentence** gives a command.
It ends with a period (.).

> Stay away from active volcanoes.
> Please be careful.

An **exclamatory sentence** shows strong feelings.
It ends with an exclamation mark (**!**).

> How amazing that would be!
> Wow, the colors are so bright!

■ Every sentence begins with a capital letter and ends with a
punctuation mark. The end punctuation you use depends on
the kind of sentence you write.

PRACTICE

A *Read each sentence. Write **declarative**, **interrogative**, **imperative**,
or **exclamatory** to tell what kind of sentence it is.*

1. What an incredible sight that is! _____

2. Hot melted rock, gas, and steam burst from the volcano. _____

3. Watch how the hot ash and lava flow down the mountain. _____

4. What is lava? _____

5. Lava is hot liquid rock that comes out of a volcano. _____

6. Wow, a lava flow looks so dangerous! _____

7. Please leave the area immediately. _____

8. One famous volcano is Mount Vesuvius in Italy. _____

9. Will Mount Vesuvius erupt again? _____

10. I hope not! _____

B Add the correct end punctuation to each sentence. Then write *declarative, interrogative, imperative,* or *exclamatory* to tell what kind of sentence it is.

1. We learned more about volcanoes _____ _____

2. Wow, they can be so destructive _____ _____

3. Fortunately, they do not erupt very often _____ _____

4. What are the warning signs of an eruption _____ _____

5. One sign is a loud explosion _____ _____

6. Hey, that was such a loud clap _____ _____

7. You really scared me _____ _____

8. Move out of the path of the lava _____ _____

9. Look at the volcanic ash _____ _____

10. Please tell me more about volcanoes _____ _____

11. What else would you like to know _____ _____

12. Are there any volcanoes in our state _____ _____

C *Here is a conversation among some friends on a hike. The dialogue has three missing capital letters and seven missing or incorrect end marks. Look for the mistakes and correct them. Use the proofreading marks in the box.*

Bianca	Mount Rainier is the highest peak in the state of Washington.
Danny	exactly how tall is it?
Bianca	Read that sign over there
Maria	Wow, it's 14,410 feet high
Bianca	we'll only climb a thousand feet or so.
Maria	What a relief that is
Danny	Wait for me, you two.
Bianca	Did you know that Mount Rainier is a volcano
Maria	Are you serious.
Bianca	the last major eruption was about 500 years ago.
Danny	Will it erupt again soon!
Bianca	The scientists say no
Maria	Let's hurry up anyway.
Danny	You can't be too careful!

Proofreading Marks

∧	Add
⊙	Period
℘	Take out
≡	Capital letter
/	Small letter

Did you correct ten mistakes with capital letters and end marks?

WRITE

D *Imagine each situation below. Write a sentence that the person might say in the situation. Write the kind of sentence that is given in parentheses. The first one is done for you.*

Situation 1 Ms. Murray is teaching about volcanoes. She makes this statement about volcanoes. (declarative)

Ms. Murray   *Hot ash or lava can erupt from a volcano.* _____

Situation 2 Your classmate Janet does not understand something about volcanoes. She raises her hand and asks a question. Write the question she asks. (interrogative)

Janet   _____

Situation 3 Lois is another classmate. She is very surprised by a fact she learns about volcanoes. Write the statement she makes to show her surprise. (exclamatory)

Lois   _____

Situation 4 Your friend Jerry hears that you have drawn some pictures of a volcano. He lets you know that he wants to look at them. Write the statement he makes. (imperative)

Jerry   _____

Situation 5 Luis thinks your drawings are really great. He wants to display them in some way. Write the question he asks. (interrogative)

Luis   _____

Proofreading Checklist ☑

❏ *Did you begin each sentence with a capital letter?*
❏ *Did you end each sentence with the correct end mark?*

Lesson 2: **Complete Subjects and Predicates**

LEARN

A **simple sentence** expresses a complete thought.
It has a subject and a predicate.

- The **subject** tells *whom* or *what* the sentence is about.
   Maggie asks many questions.

The **predicate** tells what the subject *does* or *is*.
   Maggie **asks many questions**.

- The **complete subject** includes all the words in
   the subject part of the sentence. The **complete
   predicate** includes all the words in the predicate
   part of the sentence.

The complete subject or complete predicate can be one
word or more than one word.

Complete Subject	Complete Predicate
Our little sister Maggie	smiles.
She	takes things apart.
My mom and dad	call her "the inventor."
All real inventors	are explorers.
The pictures in this book	gave us ideas.

PRACTICE

A *Read each sentence. Write **complete subject** or **complete predicate** to tell
which part of the sentence is in **boldface**. The first one is done for you.*

1. **Benjamin Franklin** was a great inventor. _____complete subject_____

2. **His inventions** are part of our everyday lives. _____

3. Ben **needed two pairs of eyeglasses**. _____

4. One pair **was for reading**. _____

5. **The other pair** was for seeing things at a distance.

_____

6. **Franklin** hated carrying two pairs of glasses.

_____

7. He **invented new glasses that solved the problem**.

_____

8. **Ben** put half of a lens for distance on top.

_____

9. He **put half of a lens for reading on the bottom**.

_____

10. We **call these glasses "bifocals."**

_____

B *Read each sentence. Draw a line between the complete subject and the complete predicate. Underline the complete subject once and the complete predicate twice. The first one is done for you.*

1. Ben Franklin|invented a new kind of stove.

2. The new stove got hot fast.

3. The new invention warmed every part of a room.

4. The Franklin stove was safer than a fire in a fireplace.

5. It burned less wood than other stoves.

6. People use Ben's stove even today.

7. Ben Franklin experimented with unusual ideas, too.

8. This busy scientist tested one idea in a pond.

9. Ben tied a kite to himself.

10. He swam in the pond.

11. The wind blew the kite.

12. The kite pulled Ben across the pond.

Franklin stove

C *Write a complete subject or a complete predicate to complete each sentence. Choose a subject or predicate from the box, or use a subject or predicate of your own. Write your sentence on the lines provided, adding the correct end punctuation.*

Remember 💡

The **complete subject** tells *whom* or *what* the sentence is about.

The **complete predicate** tells what the subject *does* or *is*.

> the gasoline engine   business and trade
>
> turned nighttime into day   let people record information
>
> early clocks   made travel much easier and safer
>
> certain inventions

1. have changed the world completely _____

_____

2. The invention of writing _____

_____

3. grew quickly after the invention of money _____

_____

4. The first maps _____

_____

5. helped people manage time better _____

_____

6. made cars and trucks possible _____

_____

7. The electric lightbulb _____

_____

WRITE

D *The computer is another invention that is changing our world. Use what you know about computers to complete each sentence. Add a complete subject or a complete predicate to each group of words. Write each sentence on the lines provided. Check a dictionary if you need help spelling a word.*

1. The invention of the computer _____

_____

2. use personal computers at home. _____

_____

3. Our school computers _____

_____

4. play games on computers. _____

_____

5. The computers in the library _____

_____

6. find information for reports and homework on the Internet. _____

_____

7. Modern cars, televisions, and music players _____

_____

8. solve problems with computers. _____

_____

Proofreading Checklist ✔

❑ *Does each sentence begin with a capital letter?*
❑ *Does each sentence end with a period or other end mark?*
❑ *Does each sentence have a subject and a predicate?*

Lesson 3: **Simple Subjects**

LEARN

■ The **simple subject** is the most important word in the complete subject. The simple subject tells exactly *whom* or *what* the subject is about.

■ Sometimes the subject of a sentence is just one word. Sometimes it is a name. Then the simple subject and the complete subject are the same. Most of the time, however, the simple subject is part of the complete subject.

In the chart below the simple subjects are shown in **boldface**.

Helen Keller sitting at a desk

Complete Subject	Complete Predicate
The school **librarian**	gave me a book.
The **book**	was about Helen Keller.
Helen Keller	lost her hearing and sight.
She	needed a special teacher.

PRACTICE

A *The complete subject in each sentence is in **boldface**. Circle the simple subject in the complete subject. Write it on the line.*

1. **This book** is about Helen Keller's remarkable life. _____

2. **Helen Keller** became ill at the age of 19 months. _____

3. **The mysterious illness** left her blind and deaf. _____

4. **Anne Sullivan** was Helen's teacher. _____

5. **The gifted teacher** taught Helen how to read and write. _____

6. **Helen** graduated from college in 1904 with Anne's help. _____

7. **The two women** traveled around the world. _____

8. The proud student told people her story. _____

9. Large audiences learned an important lesson
from her. _____

10. An independent life is possible even with
physical challenges. _____

B *Underline the complete subject in each sentence. Then circle
the simple subject, and write it on the line.*

1. Levi Strauss made the first blue jeans in the 1870s. _____

2. He was born in a part of Europe called Bavaria. _____

3. This area is now a part of Germany. _____

4. Strauss moved to New York in 1847. _____

5. Levi joined the family clothing business. _____

6. The young man brought the business to California. _____

7. Many people searched for gold in California. _____

8. The gold miners bought the pants Levi made. _____

9. A heavy blue fabric made the pants strong. _____

10. The family business expanded quickly. _____

11. Many Americans wanted the waist overalls. _____

12. "Waist overalls" was the old name for jeans. _____

C *Write a complete subject to complete each sentence. Choose a complete subject from the box, or use a complete subject of your own. Then circle the simple subject.*

 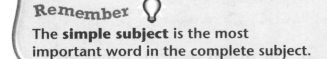
> Most readers   Exciting historical events
>
> The person   A biography   Everyday events

_____ tells the story of a

person's life. _____ might be an

artist, an athlete, or a president. _____

enjoy biographies very much. _____

come alive in a well-written biography. _____

can be interesting, too.

> A biographer   These written records
>
> The actual writing   Most authors   Research

_____ work very hard on biographies.

_____ is the first part of their job.

_____ must read old letters, diaries, and

news stories about a person. _____ reveal

a great deal about the person. _____ can

take years and years.

WRITE

Sometimes two related sentences have the same predicate.

Lena read a biography of Harriet Tubman.
Her friend read a biography of Harriet Tubman.

When this happens you can combine the subjects and form one sentence. Use the word *and* to join the subjects. Combining the sentences in this way will make your writing smoother.

Lena **and** her friend read a biography of Harriet Tubman.

D *Each pair of sentences below has the same predicate. Combine the sentences by joining the subjects.*

1. Harriet Tubman lived in slavery. Her family lived in slavery. _____

_____

2. Hardship shaped their lives. Struggles shaped their lives. _____

_____

3. Harriet Tubman escaped. Her parents escaped. _____

_____

4. Slave owners looked for Tubman. The police looked for Tubman. _____

_____

5. Tubman never got caught. The slaves with her never got caught. _____

_____

6. Careful planning led to her success. Quick thinking led to her success. _____

_____

Go back to the sentences you wrote.
Underline the subjects you combined.
Circle the word that joins them.

Lesson 4: **Simple Predicates**

LEARN

- The **simple predicate** is the most important word in the complete predicate. The simple predicate tells exactly what the subject *does* or *is*.

- Sometimes the predicate of a sentence is just one word. Then the simple predicate and the complete predicate are the same. Most of the time, however, the simple predicate is part of the complete predicate.

In the chart below, the simple predicates are shown in **boldface**.

Complete Subject	Complete Predicate
Everyone	**read**.
All of us	**searched** for information.
Our class	**planned** a trip to Ellis Island.
Ellis Island	**is** in New York City.
We	**rode** a ferry to the island.
Many tourists	**visit** the immigration museum.

PRACTICE

A *The complete predicate in each sentence is in **boldface**. Circle the simple predicate in the complete predicate. Write it on the line.*

1. This small island **is in New York Harbor.** _____

2. Samuel Ellis **owned the island at one time.** _____

3. The federal government **built a fort there in 1811.** _____

4. The fort **became an immigrant center in 1892.** _____

5. Immigrants **went there for inspections.** _____

6. The government **used the center for 62 years.** _____

7. Ellis Island **closed officially in November 1954.** _____

8. A new project **began in 1984.** _____

9. The Island **reopened as a museum.** _____

10. Over a million people **visit the museum each year.** _____

B *Underline the complete predicate in each sentence. Then circle the simple predicate, and write it on the line.*

1. Huge numbers of immigrants came to New York City. _____

2. About eight million entered the city from 1855 to 1890. _____

3. Many groups arrived at Ellis Island. _____

4. Most people left poor conditions back home. _____

5. The newcomers wanted better lives in America. _____

6. Some immigrants brought family members with them. _____

7. Others traveled by themselves. _____

8. Many immigrants crossed the ocean by steamship. _____

9. The ships docked at the piers. _____

10. Doctors examined the immigrants for illnesses. _____

11. Inspectors requested the proper papers. _____

12. Some passengers got special treatment. _____

13. Officials checked them aboard the ships. _____

14. The inspections lasted for hours. _____

15. Most immigrants passed inspection. _____

C Write a complete predicate to complete each sentence in this diary entry. Choose a complete predicate from the box, or use a complete predicate of your own. Then circle the simple predicate.

asked us lots of questions

showed us our new home

cried with happiness

was over at last

carried us to my uncle's apartment

held her torch high above us

took us to Ellis Island

Dear Diary,

Today our ship steamed into New York Harbor. The beautiful Statue of Liberty _____.

My mother and I _____. Our long voyage _____!

A small ferry _____. There the officials _____. Finally, we were free to go.

An underground train _____.

He _____. Our new life in America is beginning at last!

WRITE

Sometimes two related sentences have the same subject.

> Mom studied history.
> Mom shared what she knew.

When this happens you can combine the predicates and form one sentence. Use the word *and* to join the predicates. Combining the sentences in this way will make your writing smoother.

> Mom <u>studied history</u> **and** <u>shared what she knew</u>.

D *Each pair of sentences below has the same subject. Combine the sentences by joining the predicates.*

1. The United States changed. The United States grew. _____

_____

2. Millions of immigrants left Europe. Millions of immigrants came here. _____

_____

3. A father often came first. A father sent for his family later. _____

_____

4. The immigrants usually lived in big cities. The immigrants worked in jobs there.

_____

_____

5. New York City had the most immigrants. New York City became the largest city.

_____

_____

Go back to the sentences you wrote.
Underline the predicates you combined.
Circle the word that joins them.

Lesson 5: Compound Sentences

LEARN

- A **simple sentence** has one subject and one predicate. It expresses one idea.

  The National Zoo is in Washington, D.C.

- Sometimes two simple sentences contain related ideas. You can combine these sentences to make a **compound sentence**. Use a connecting word such as *and*, *but*, or *or* to join the sentences.

  RELATED SENTENCES
  The National Zoo is huge. It has animals from all over the world.

  COMPOUND SENTENCE
  The National Zoo is huge, **and** it has animals from all over the world.

  RELATED SENTENCES
  Most zoos do not have pandas. The National Zoo does.

  COMPOUND SENTENCE
  Most zoos do not have pandas, **but** the National Zoo does.

  RELATED SENTENCES
  Would you like to go to the zoo? Would you rather see a movie?

  COMPOUND SENTENCE
  Would you like to go to the zoo, **or** would you rather see a movie?

The connecting words *and*, *but*, and *or* are called **coordinating conjunctions**. A comma (,) always goes before the conjunction in a compound sentence.

PRACTICE

A *Read each sentence. Write **simple** if the sentence is made up of only one idea. Write **compound** if the sentence is made up of two related ideas.*

1. Pandas feed mostly on bamboo plants. _____

2. A panda's head is white, but its eyes and ears are black. _____

3. Are pandas in the raccoon family, or are they true bears? _____

4. Pandas are endangered, but people are working to protect them.   _____

5. Grizzly bears walk slowly, but they can run fast.   _____

6. Grizzlies eat many kinds of plants, and they eat fish, too.   _____

7. A polar bear's coat is waterproof.   _____

8. Polar bears are excellent swimmers.   _____

9. Black bears are commonly found in the eastern United States.   _____

10. Keep away from black bears, or you might get hurt.   _____

B *Read each incomplete compound sentence. Underline the sentence below that best relates to it. Then combine the related sentences to form a compound sentence. Write the compound sentence on the line.*

1. Adult pandas weigh several hundred pounds, but _____.
Pandas are in the bear family.   Newborns weigh just one pound.

_____

2. Brown bears eat meat, or _____.
The tips of their hairs are white.   They eat plants, insects, and fish.

_____

3. Grizzly cubs can climb trees, but _____.
Adult grizzlies cannot.   They like honey.

_____

4. Polar bears live near the water, and _____.
They have small ears.   They hunt seals there.

_____

5. A brown bear has a shoulder hump, and _____.
Grizzly bears are brown bears.   It has very long claws.

_____

C *One zoo posted this list of rules for visitors. The compound sentences on the list have six mistakes. Look for the mistakes and correct them. Use the proofreading marks in the box.*

ZOO RULES

Enjoy your visit! Our zoo is a wonderful place to explore and these rules will keep you safe and happy.

- Please don't feed the animals. Our animals have special diets and human food can make them sick.

- Pets are not allowed at the zoo but guide dogs are permitted.

- Railings and fences protect you and they also keep our animals safe. Never extend fingers and arms through fences.

- Visitors may carry personal digital devices but they must use headphones. Noise can disturb both animals and people.

- Don't litter. Place all your trash in the bins or our zoo won't be a pleasant place to visit.

Proofreading Marks

∧	Add
⊙	Period
ℒ	Take out
≡	Capital letter
/	Small letter

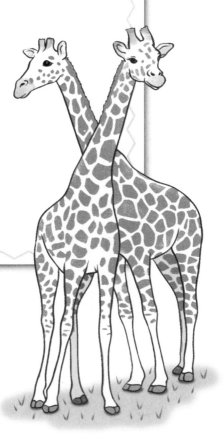

 Did you correct six mistakes in the compound sentences?

WRITE

D *Each pair of sentences below contains related ideas. Combine the sentences to form a compound sentence. Use the coordinating conjunction in parentheses to join them. Remember to put a comma before the joining word. The first one is done for you.*

1. Zookeepers know more about how an animal lives. They build better zoos. (and)

Zookeepers know more about how an animal lives, and they build better zoos.

2. Animals move around freely. People can still get a good view of them. (but)

_____

_____

3. Conditions must be just right in a zoo. Animals get sick. (or) _____

_____

4. Polar bears need icy cold water. Lions need warm temperatures. (but) _____

_____

5. Zoo animals need to stay busy. They will become bored and unhappy. (or)

_____

_____

6. Apes search for their own food in today's zoos. Some zoo elephants even paint

pictures. (and) _____

_____

7. The field feels as if it is the giraffes' natural home. There is lots of room to roam.

(and) _____

_____

8. Modern zoos are difficult to build and run. They're worth it. (but) _____

_____

Lesson 6: **Complex Sentences**

LEARN

- You have learned about compound sentences. Compound sentences combine related ideas using a connecting word such as *and*, *but*, or *or*.

  A **complex sentence** also combines related ideas. The ideas are joined by a **subordinating conjunction**. Look at the sentence below.

  The canyon is wide **because** the river has eroded its walls.

  The subordinating conjunction *because* joins the two related ideas.

The following **subordinating conjunctions** are often used to connect related ideas.

Subordinating Conjunctions			
after	although	because	before
since	until	when	while

- The subordinating conjunction may come in the middle of the sentence.
  Plains are mostly flat **although** some have small hills.

- The subordinating conjunction may come at the beginning of the sentence.
  Although some have small hills, plains are mostly flat.

  Notice that when the first idea in the sentence begins with a subordinating conjunction, a comma follows that idea.

PRACTICE

A *Read each sentence. Write **complex** if the sentence is made up of two related ideas joined by a subordinating conjunction. Write **not complex** if it is not a complex sentence.*

1. After we made the last turn, we reached the mountain. _____

2. We wanted to see the mountain because it is so majestic. _____

3. A mountain is higher than the area around it. _____

4. The taller mountains reach into the colder layers of
the atmosphere.   _____

5. Since the mountain slope is gentle, it is perfect for skiing.   _____

6. Mountains take millions of years to form.   _____

7. A mountain can form when Earth's crust bends.   _____

8. Unlike mountains the plains are low and flat.   _____

9. Because they are low-lying areas, plains can flood easily.   _____

10. Plains may be surrounded by small hills or mountains.   _____

B *Read each complex sentence. Write the subordinating conjunction that joins the two related ideas. The first one is done for you.*

1. When an earthquake happens, you can take steps
to be safe.   _____*When*_____

2. You should take cover until the ground stops shaking.   _____

3. Since earthquakes sometimes happen under the ocean,
you may see waves on the surface.   _____

4. A tsunami can take place after an earthquake strikes.   _____

5. Some cities are prepared for an earthquake because
they have had so many.   _____

6. Although some earthquakes are dangerous, most are not.   _____

7. Scientists could study an earthquake better when they
had the latest tools.   _____

8. Before an earthquake hits, some animals seem nervous.   _____

9. We saw a wide crack in the ground while we
were hiking.   _____

10. The ground cracked because parts of the earth had
split apart.   _____

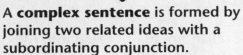

C *Write a subordinating conjunction to complete each sentence. Choose a subordinating conjunction from the box, or use a subordinating conjunction of your own.*

Remember 💡

A **complex sentence** is formed by joining two related ideas with a subordinating conjunction.

after	although	because	before
since	until	when	while

1. Thomas went to Costa Rica _____ he wanted to see a volcano.

2. _____ I have read about volcanoes, I haven't seen one.

3. Thomas showed us his photographs _____ he returned from his trip.

4. _____ she is a park ranger at Denali National Park, Aunt Mary can tell us about glaciers.

5. Glaciers leave rocks behind _____ they move across the land.

6. _____ we traveled to Alaska last spring, I had never seen a glacier.

7. I read books about glaciers _____ we took our trip.

8. I saw one of these large sheets of ice

_____ our plane landed.

9. I put on a heavy coat _____ it is cold on top of a glacier.

10. _____ there once were many glaciers in America, there are few today.

11. _____ some glaciers contain a lot of air, they can look blue.

12. We heard loud noises _____ pieces of a glacier broke off.

WRITE

D *Imagine a beautiful island that you want people to visit. Use the items below to create a persuasive article about the island. Be sure to use complete sentences. Check a dictionary if you need help spelling a word.*

1. because the island is far away

_____

_____

2. after you arrive _____

_____

3. since so much water surrounds the island _____

_____

4. when you are at the beach _____

_____

5. although there is a volcano _____

_____

6. until you see the amazing flowers here _____

_____

7. while you are at the beach _____

_____

8. before you leave _____

_____

Proofreading Checklist ☑

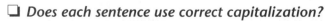

❑ *Does each sentence use correct capitalization?*
❑ *Does each sentence that begins with a subordinating conjunction have a comma after the first idea?*

Lesson 7: Correcting Fragments and Run-ons

LEARN

- A **fragment** is an incomplete sentence. The subject or predicate might be missing. To correct this kind of fragment, add a subject or a predicate.

FRAGMENT	Bought a children's book.
SENTENCE	My sister bought a children's book.

⌐↑___**Add a subject.**

FRAGMENT	The book.
SENTENCE	The book is for my brother.

Add a predicate.___↑

- A **run-on sentence** is two complete sentences that run together. One way to correct a run-on sentence is to make two separate sentences. Another way is to make a compound sentence.

RUN-ON
She likes to draw she wants to be an artist.

CORRECTED SENTENCE
She likes to draw. She wants to be an artist.

↑___**two separate sentences**

CORRECTED SENTENCE
She likes to draw, and she wants to be an artist.

↑___**compound sentence**

PRACTICE

A *Read each group of words. Circle **sentence**, **fragment**, or **run-on** to describe it.*

1. Lane Smith is an illustrator.   *sentence*   *fragment*   *run-on*

2. The young artist.   *sentence*   *fragment*   *run-on*

3. He loved to draw pictures he loved baseball.   *sentence*   *fragment*   *run-on*

4. He is grateful to his teachers.   *sentence*   *fragment*   *run-on*

5. They encouraged him they helped him.   *sentence*   *fragment*   *run-on*

6. One of his teachers.   *sentence*   *fragment*   *run-on*

7. Tried out different art supplies.   *sentence*   *fragment*   *run-on*

8. This artist has a great imagination.   *sentence*   *fragment*   *run-on*

B *Make each fragment a complete sentence by matching it with the correct subject or predicate. Write the letter of the words you choose on the line.*

_____ **1.** *The Tale of Peter Rabbit*   **a.** is Beatrix Potter.

_____ **2.** The author's name   **b.** is a well-known children's book.

_____ **3.** wrote the story in a letter.   **c.** The letter

_____ **4.** was for a little boy who was sick.   **d.** later turned the story into a book.

_____ **5.** Potter   **e.** Beatrix

Write each run-on sentence as a compound sentence.

6. Beatrix Potter made the story longer she redrew the pictures, too. _____

_____

7. She wanted to make books for children she wanted to make them easy to hold.

_____

8. Beatrix made the books little she used sturdy paper. _____

_____

Write each run-on sentence as two separate sentences.

9. Beatrix Potter grew up in England drawing was her favorite hobby.

_____

10. Beatrix had a younger brother both children loved plants and animals.

_____

C Leah wrote this report. It contains three fragments and three run-on sentences. Use the proofreading marks in the box to correct the mistakes. Add a subject or predicate to correct each fragment. Write each run-on sentence as a compound sentence or as two separate sentences.

Remember

A **fragment** is an incomplete sentence.

A **run-on sentence** is two complete sentences that run together.

Thousands of children's books are published each year most of them have good illustrations. However, only one book gets the Caldecott Medal. Goes to the best illustrator of a children's book.

The Caldecott Medal is a very special honor. The American Library Association presents the award. Librarians study the year's new children's books, they vote on the best one.

The first Caldecott Medal was given in 1938. Since then many great illustrators have won it. Encourages artists to draw fine pictures for young readers.

Sometimes you might see a gold Caldecott Medal on a book. This medal. Take a minute to look inside it you're sure to find some outstanding illustrations.

Proofreading Marks

∧	Add
⊙	Period
ℓ	Take out
≡	Capital letter
/	Small letter

Did you correct three fragments and three run-on sentences?

WRITE

D *Add a subject or predicate to each fragment to make a complete sentence. Write the sentence on the line.*

1. A book's illustrations. _____

_____

2. Add interest to the story. _____

_____

3. Show the mood and feelings in a story, too. _____

_____

4. Drawings, paintings, and photographs. _____

_____

5. Photographs. _____

_____

6. My favorite book illustrator. _____

_____

7. The Caldecott Medal. _____

_____

8. Are fun to read. _____

_____

9. Books without illustrations. _____

_____

10. Are on display in the library. _____

_____

Kinds of Sentences (pp. 8–11) *Read each sentence.*
Write declarative, interrogative, imperative, or exclamatory
to tell what kind of sentence it is.

1. A tornado hit the town yesterday. _____

2. Did you see the tornado? _____

3. Look at these photos. _____

4. How lucky we were! _____

Complete Subjects and Predicates (pp. 12–15)
Read each sentence. Draw a line between the complete subject and
the complete predicate. Underline the complete subject once and the
complete predicate twice.

5. A tornado looks like a dark funnel-shaped cloud.

6. Winds whirl around at high speeds.

7. These dangerous storms move in a narrow path across the earth.

8. The twisting cloud picks up dirt from the ground.

Simple Subjects (pp. 16–19) *Read each sentence. Underline the*
complete subject. Then circle the simple subject.

9. About 700 tornadoes occur in the United States each year.

10. These powerful storms damage everything in their path.

11. The gusty winds uproot trees.

12. Some automobiles fly through the air for hundreds of feet.

Simple Predicates (pp. 20–23) *Read each sentence. Underline the*
complete predicate. Then circle the simple predicate.

13. Most tornadoes hit the midwestern states.

14. Certain weather conditions produce these storms.

15. Weather scientists track tornadoes.

16. The scientists announce tornado warnings whenever possible.

Compound Sentences (pp. 24–27) *Read each sentence.*
Write **simple** *if the sentence is made up of only one idea.*
Write **compound** *if the sentence is made up of two related ideas.*

17. Most tornadoes occur on hot and humid days. _____

18. Warm air rises rapidly, and sometimes it begins to spin. _____

19. This spinning air sometimes forms a tornado. _____

20. The tornado can stay in the air, or it might touch
down on the ground. _____

Complex Sentences (pp. 28–31) *Read each sentence.*
Write **complex** *if it is a complex sentence. Write* **not complex**
if it is not a complex sentence.

21. Although most tornadoes last only a few minutes,
they can cause great damage. _____

22. The Fujita scale, or F-scale, measures a tornado's intensity. _____

23. An F5 rating on the F-scale stands for the greatest
wind strength any tornado can have. _____

24. A tornado warning will be issued when radar spots
powerful winds. _____

Correcting Fragments and Run-ons (pp. 32–35) *Read each*
group of words. Write **sentence, fragment,** *or* **run-on** *to describe it.*

25. A storm cellar gives the best protection from a
tornado a basement is the next safest place. _____

26. The National Weather Service. _____

27. Always keep away from windows during a tornado. _____

28. Warns people about tornadoes. _____

TIP 💡
Remember, you can find out more
about sentences on pages 8–35.

PROOFREADING PRACTICE

*Read the text below. There are 15 mistakes in the use of sentences. Use the
proofreading marks in the box to correct them.*

Proofreading Marks	
∧	Add
⊙	Period
ℰ	Take out
≡	Capital letter
/	Small letter

I woke up on Saturday morning to sunlight streaming
through my window We were going to the park for a
picnic and I needed to get ready fast.

We arrived, the park was already crowded. Groups
of kids played soccer on the sports fields. Blankets
were spread all over the grass. Were reading or napping on them.

"Mom, there's no room for us" I exclaimed. She frowned
slightly, her expression quickly changed into a smile.

"Do you hear that music, Maya" Mom asked as her eyes lit up.
"Let's find out where it's coming from!"

we strolled along a path. As we approached the middle of the
park, the music got louder. A singer, guitarist, and drummer. Were
holding a concert on a tiny stage.

"Should we sit down, should we dance?" Mom asked
mischievously. We began moving to the music. soon, everyone
around us was dancing, too. Music was all we needed to have a
fantastic day at the park

WRITE ABOUT IT

Write a story about someone else who goes to the same concert in the park. Use details from the text on page 38. Include a variety of sentences in your story. Use the Writing Process Handbook on pages 236–251 to help you plan. When you are finished writing your draft, then proofread your work.

_____

_____

_____

_____

_____

_____

_____

_____

Check It Out! ✔

Did you . . .
- ❏ *write a story about someone else who goes to the concert in the park?*
- ❏ *use details from the text on page 38 in your story?*
- ❏ *include a variety of sentences in your story?*
- ❏ *revise and edit your writing to show what you learned about sentences?*
- ❏ *proofread for correct spelling, capitalization, and punctuation?*

TALK ABOUT IT

Discuss: *When was the last time you visited a park? Whom did you go with? What did you do there? Use a variety of sentences to talk about your experience.*

Lesson 8: Common and Proper Nouns

LEARN

- A **noun** is a word that names a person, place, or thing.
  A **common noun** names any person, place, or thing.
  The **girl** visited the **fountain** in the **park**.

- A **proper noun** names a specific person, place, or thing.
  It can be one word or more than one word.
  Julia visited **Bethesda Fountain** in **Central Park**.

- Each important word in a proper noun begins with
  a capital letter.

	Common	Proper
Person	teacher	Ms. Jones
Place	city	Los Angeles
Thing	statue	Statue of Liberty

Bethesda Fountain in
Central Park

- Ideas such as *fear* and *greed* are called **abstract nouns**.
  You can't see or touch them, but they are still nouns.
  Abstract nouns are always common nouns.
  Greed was his undoing.

PRACTICE

A *Match each common noun with a proper noun. Write the letter of the proper noun on the line.*

Common Nouns

_____ **1.** month

_____ **2.** country

Proper Nouns

a. Mexico

b. October

_____ **3.** holiday

_____ **4.** planet

_____ **5.** building

_____ **6.** state

_____ **7.** continent

_____ **8.** day of the week

_____ **9.** lake

_____ **10.** president

c. Venus

d. Fourth of July

e. White House

f. Asia

g. Abraham Lincoln

h. Nebraska

i. Monday

j. Lake Charles

B *Read each sentence. Write **common** if the noun in **boldface** is a common noun. Write **proper** if it is a proper noun.*

1. Dora visited **Yellowstone National Park** last summer. _____

2. The **park** lies mainly in Wyoming. _____

3. Is it the largest national park in the **United States**? _____

4. The park's geysers attract many **visitors**. _____

5. Water from inside the earth shoots out of a **geyser**. _____

6. **Old Faithful** is the most famous geyser. _____

7. Spectators feel great **excitement** when this geyser erupts. _____

8. People visit the **Mammoth Hot Springs**, too. _____

9. **Dora** hiked up to Yellowstone Lake. _____

10. Her **love** of Yellowstone is apparent. _____

C Dora wrote this letter to her grandmother. She made twelve mistakes when writing common and proper nouns. Look for the mistakes and fix them. Use the proofreading marks in the box.

Dear Grandma,

Can you imagine a Canyon 18 miles wide and a mile deep? Well, if you were here in Grand Canyon national Park in arizona, you wouldn't have to. You could be hiking in it with us!

The Trip is not all hiking, though. On tuesday we rafted down the Colorado river for about 10 Miles! We only got wet twice, and we got to see some Sheep. We might take a mule Trip tomorrow to a place called Phantom ranch. That sounds scary, but I still want to go.

We will be home by september 1st, and I will see you at our picnic on Labor day. I can't wait to tell you more about the trip!

Love,

Dora

Proofreading Marks

∧	Add
⊙	Period
ℰ	Take out
≡	Capital letter
/	Small letter

 Did you correct twelve mistakes?

WRITE

Sometimes your sentences might have nouns that are not clear or specific.

> Our train travels along the **river**.
> We can see **boats** on the water.

You can replace these nouns with nouns that are more descriptive. The words you choose can be either common or proper nouns.

> Our train travels along the **Hudson River**.
> We can see **sailboats** on the water.

D *In each sentence below change the word or words in **boldface** to a more descriptive noun. Use either a common noun or a proper noun. Write the new sentence on the line.*

1. I would like to visit **a city** some day.

_____

2. There is a really famous **thing** there.

_____

3. I will probably invite **a friend** to go with me.

_____

4. We could pack **food** for lunch.

_____

5. We will bring some **fruit** for snacktime, too.

_____

6. We would send postcards to **a teacher**.

_____

7. During the trip home we would play **a game**.

_____

Go back to the sentences you wrote.
Circle the more descriptive nouns you used.

Lesson 9: Singular and Plural Nouns

LEARN

■ Nouns can be singular or plural. A **singular noun** names one person, place, or thing. A **plural noun** names more than one person, place, or thing.

| SINGULAR | I visited an **exhibit** at the county fair. |
| PLURAL | I visited three **exhibits** at the county fair. |

■ Follow these rules to make plural nouns.

• **Add -s to most singular nouns.**

| SINGULAR | bird | bee | flower | vegetable |
| PLURAL | bird**s** | bee**s** | flower**s** | vegetable**s** |

• **Add -es when a singular noun ends in s, ss, ch, sh, or x.**

| SINGULAR | bus | dress | porch | dish | ax |
| PLURAL | bus**es** | dress**es** | porch**es** | dish**es** | ax**es** |

• **When a singular noun ends in a vowel and y, add -s.**

| SINGULAR | boy | key | holiday |
| PLURAL | boy**s** | key**s** | holiday**s** |

• **When a singular noun ends in a consonant and y, change the y to i and add -es.**

| SINGULAR | lady | family | cherry |
| PLURAL | lad**ies** | famil**ies** | cherr**ies** |

PRACTICE

A *Write the plural form of each noun.*

1. wish _____

2. bunny _____

3. patch _____

4. donkey _____

5. tax _____

6. celebration _____

7. guess _____

8. song _____

9. party _____

10. fox _____

B *Write the plural form of the noun in parentheses to complete each sentence.*

1. Many _____ in our state hold fairs each summer. (county)

2. Different farm _____ help pay for the events. (group)

3. Tourists arrive in cars and _____. (bus)

4. The _____ at the fair are always interesting. (event)

5. Some _____ sell products to the visitors. (business)

6. _____ of prize-winning fruits and vegetables fill one building. (box)

7. The apples and _____ always look delicious. (peach)

8. You can sample the homemade jams and _____. (jelly)

9. _____ of fresh-squeezed juice are on sale, too. (glass)

10. _____ made with local cheeses are popular. (sandwich)

11. Most children and _____ love the animal exhibits. (baby)

12. Horses and _____ fill one huge barn. (pony)

13. Visitors look at the colorful chickens and _____. (turkey)

14. The best cows and sheep win blue ribbons for _____. (prize)

15. We look forward to the fair for _____. (month)

C *Ron wrote this report. He made nine mistakes when writing nouns. Sometimes he misspelled plural nouns. At other times he used a plural noun for a singular noun or a singular noun for a plural noun. Use the proofreading marks to correct these mistakes.*

Proofreading Marks

∧	Add
⊙	Period
ℒ	Take out
≡	Capital letter
/	Small letter

Many communitys today celebrate *Cinco de Mayo.* These words are Spanish for the "Fifth of May." On May 5, 1862, the Mexican army defeated a much larger French army. The Mexican people were proud of this important victory, and the day became a holidays.

Cinco de Mayo celebrates Mexican history and culture. In some large city, official organize a big fiesta, or festival. In Los Angeles almost a million residents attend. Boy and girls in colorful costumees perform folk dances. Bands play traditional music. Different business prepare Mexican dishs for the crowd. Parades are also usually part of the big day.

Cinco de Mayo is a great way for familys and neighbors to remember their heritage and have fun, too!

Did you correct nine mistakes with nouns?

WRITE

Singular and plural nouns can appear in the subject or the predicate of a sentence. Sometimes you can combine two related sentences by joining the nouns. Use the conjunction *and* or *or* to join the nouns.

Cowboys ride in the rodeo.
Cowgirls ride in the rodeo.
Cowboys **and** cowgirls ride in the rodeo.

The rodeo will take place in the United States.
The rodeo will take place in Canada.
The rodeo will take place in the United States **or** Canada.

D *Combine each pair of sentences by joining nouns in the subject or predicate. Use the conjunction in parentheses to join the nouns.*

1. Rodeo is based on traditions from the United States. Rodeo is based

on traditions from Mexico. (and) _____

_____

2. The events developed from chores on ranches. The events developed

from activities on ranches. (and) _____

_____

3. Rodeo riders enter contests. Rodeo riders enter races. (or) _____

_____

4. The cowboys might perform first. The cowgirls might perform first. (or) _____

_____

5. Audiences enjoy the action. Audiences enjoy the excitement. (and) _____

_____

Look back at the sentences you wrote. Underline the nouns you joined in the subject or predicate.

Lesson 10: **Irregular Plural Nouns**

LEARN

- Some nouns have **irregular plurals**. In most cases the spelling of the singular noun changes to form the plural.

SINGULAR	man	woman	child	tooth
PLURAL	men	women	children	teeth

SINGULAR	foot	goose	mouse	ox
PLURAL	feet	geese	mice	oxen

- In a few cases the plural noun and the singular noun are the same.

SINGULAR	One **deer** nibbles the grass.
PLURAL	Three **deer** stand and watch.

SINGULAR	This **sheep** is white.
PLURAL	The other two **sheep** are brown.

SINGULAR	A **moose** swam across the lake.
PLURAL	Several **moose** live on the island.

PRACTICE

A *Read each sentence. Write **singular** if the noun in **boldface** is a singular noun. Write **plural** if it is a plural noun.*

1. The **children** in our class went to the wildlife refuge. _____

2. A friendly **man** met us at the entrance. _____

3. Several Canada **geese** were swimming in the pond. _____

4. A single **moose** stood at the water's edge. _____

5. We were as quiet as **mice**, but it still ran away. _____

6. Two **women** showed us a tree cut down by a beaver. _____

7. What sharp **teeth** that beaver must have! _____

8. At sunset a **deer** came down to the water to drink. _____

9. Three other **deer** soon followed. _____

10. An **ox** stood alone in the field. _____

B *Write the plural form of the noun in parentheses to complete each sentence.*

1. Twelve _____ are honking in the sky above. (goose)

2. Three _____ look up at the big birds. (woman)

3. A group of _____ is eating from a bush. (deer)

4. The animals use their _____ to tear the leaves. (tooth)

5. Several _____ chewed the bark from this young tree. (mouse)

6. Many tiny _____ left prints in the mud. (foot)

7. The four _____ point with excitement across the lake. (child)

8. Two huge _____ are standing on the other side. (moose)

9. At a farm museum two _____ tell us about the past. (man)

10. Two _____ pull a plow in a field. (ox)

11. A flock of _____ grazes in a meadow nearby. (sheep)

12. A family of _____ races across the field. (mouse)

C *Connie wrote this poem about the first day of spring. She made six mistakes when forming irregular plural nouns. Look for the mistakes and fix them. Use the proofreading marks in the box.*

The First Day of Spring

The first day of spring can't be beat!

I smile at all the people I meet.

The other childs are smiling, too.

We all go together to the zoo.

The reindeers and lions are having fun.

They all seem glad that winter is done.

The bighorn sheeps don't say, "Baa," today.

Instead they're yelling, "Hip, Hip, Hooray!"

Up in the sky six gooses are squawking.

It almost sounds as if they're talking

About spring to the mans and womens below,

But what they're saying, we'll never know.

Proofreading Marks

∧	Add
⊙	Period
ℛ	Take out
≡	Capital letter
/	Small letter

Did you correct six irregular plural nouns?

WRITE

D *Read these rhymes about irregular plural nouns. Then write three rhymes of your own. Use the words in parentheses in your rhymes.*

One bird is a goose,
And two are called geese.
But the plural of moose
Can never be meese!

The singular is man,
The plural is men.
But the plural of pan
Just cannot be pen!

1. _____ (foot)

_____ (feet)

_____ (boot)

_____ (beet)

2. _____ (ox)

_____ (oxen)

_____ (fox)

_____ (foxen)

3. _____ (mouse)

_____ (mice)

_____ (blouse)

_____ (blice)

Proofreading Checklist ✓

❑ *Did you use the words in parentheses in your rhymes?*
❑ *Did you spell the real singular and plural nouns correctly?*

Lesson 11: **Possessive Nouns**

LEARN

A **possessive noun** is a noun that shows *who* or *what* has something.

> **Janet's** mother teaches quilting.
> She displayed the **students'** quilts.

Both singular and plural nouns can be made possessive.

- To make a singular noun possessive, add an apostrophe and *-s*.

SINGULAR	Janet	family	class
SINGULAR POSSESSIVE	Janet**'s**	family**'s**	class**'s**

- To make a plural noun that ends in *-s* possessive, add only an apostrophe.

PLURAL	students	families	classes
PLURAL POSSESSIVE	students**'**	families**'**	classes**'**

- To make a plural noun that does not end in *-s* possessive, add an apostrophe and *-s*.

PLURAL	women	children	sheep
PLURAL POSSESSIVE	women**'s**	children**'s**	sheep**'s**

PRACTICE

A *Write the possessive form of the noun in **boldface**.*

1. the tools owned by the **workers**   the _____ tools

2. the hats belonging to the **men**   the _____ hats

3. the rugs belonging to the **museum**   the _____ rugs

4. the sizes of the **frames**   the _____ sizes

5. the clay belonging to the **potter**   the _____ clay

6. the quilt owned by **Mia**   _____ quilt

7. the smocks used by the **painters**　　　　the _____ smocks

8. the purchases of the **tourists**　　　　the _____ purchases

9. the design of the **building**　　　　the _____ design

10. the collection owned by **Gus**　　　　_____ collection

B Write the possessive form of the noun in parentheses that correctly completes each sentence.

1. Our _____ first craft fair was a great success. (town)

2. Our _____ projects were on display. (neighbors)

3. Some _____ embroidered pillows were in the show. (women)

4. _____ hand-carved chairs attracted a crowd. (Mr. Moss)

5. His birdhouses attracted the _____ attention. (children)

6. _____ aunt is a weaver. (Sharon)

7. She uses wool from a local _____ sheep. (farmer)

8. The _____ wool is soft. (sheep)

9. A _____ wheel turned slowly in one area. (potter)

10. A _____ hands slowly shaped clay into a vase. (man)

11. The _____ shape was almost perfect! (vase)

12. All the artists answered _____ questions. (visitors)

C *David wrote about a class trip to a glassblower's workshop. He made seven mistakes when writing possessive nouns. Look for the mistakes, and fix them. Use the proofreading marks in the box.*

Our classs visit to Ms. Andersons' glass workshop was really interesting. I especially enjoyed the glassblowing demonstration. It gave everyone a firsthand look at this artists' amazing skills.

The workshops furnace heated some glass until it melted. When the mixtures temperature was about 2000°F, Ms. Anderson briefly dipped a hollow iron blowpipe into it. A small amount of melted glass stuck to the blowpipes tip.

Ms. Anderson then blew gently into the blowpipe. Her breath forced the glass to bulge out and form a hollow bulb. With a few twists and turns, the glass'es final shape appeared. It was now a beautiful vase.

Of all the crafts I have seen so far, handmade glass fascinates me the most.

Proofreading Marks

∧	Add
⊙	Period
ℐ	Take out
≡	Capital letter
/	Small letter

Did you correct seven possessive nouns?

WRITE

D *Rewrite each phrase using a possessive noun. Then write a sentence using the new phrase. The first one is done for you.*

1. the bright colors of the quilt _____ *the quilt's bright colors* _____

The quilt's bright colors will make the room look cheerful. _____

2. the unusual shape of the basket _____

_____

3. the bird feeder belonging to our class _____

_____

4. the clubhouse of the members _____

_____

5. the sweater belonging to the baby _____

_____

6. the workshop of a blacksmith _____

_____

7. the rocking horse of the toy makers _____

_____

8. the needle of the sewing machine _____

_____

Proofreading Checklist ✓

❑ *Did you make singular nouns possessive by adding an apostrophe and -s?*

❑ *Did you make plural nouns ending in -s possessive by adding just an apostrophe?*

Common and Proper Nouns (pp. 40–43) *Read each sentence.*
Write **common** *if the noun in* **boldface** *is a common noun.*
Write **proper** *if it is a proper noun.*

1. The town of **Plymouth** is in Massachusetts. _____

2. Settlers called **Pilgrims** built the town. _____

3. **Native Americans** lived nearby. _____

4. Together they celebrated a harvest **festival**. _____

5. The Pilgrims set up long **tables** outdoors. _____

6. Today **actors** dress up as the Pilgrims in Plymouth. _____

7. They act out the first **Thanksgiving**. _____

8. At the first Thanksgiving, the Pilgrim's showed their
   appreciation for the plentiful harvest. _____

Singular and Plural Nouns (pp. 44–47) *Read each sentence.*
Write the plural form of the noun in parentheses.

9. Most American (family) celebrate Thanksgiving. _____

10. Traditional (dish) are important in this feast. _____

11. Stores sell many (turkey) for the main meal. _____

12. (Box) of pies are piled up on shelves. _____

13. (Cranberry) are another specialty of the day. _____

14. Cooks use them to make (sauce) and relishes. _____

15. Guests arrive from faraway towns and (city). _____

16. Some (community) have Thanksgiving Day parades. _____

Irregular Plural Nouns (pp. 48–51) *Read each sentence. Write the plural of the noun in parentheses.*

17. There were ten (child) at our Thanksgiving dinner.

18. The dining room table was over 16 (foot) long.

19. All the men and (woman) helped cook the meal.

20. I couldn't wait to sink my (tooth) into the turkey!

21. Later we went outside and saw a flock of (goose).

22. I asked if a group of (sheep) is also called a flock.

23. I think a group of (deer) would be a herd.

24. Ben wanted to know what to call a group of (moose).

Possessive Nouns (pp. 52–55) *Read each sentence. Write the possessive form of the noun in parentheses.*

25. Have you ever heard (Sarah Hale) name before?

26. She called attention to (Thanksgiving) importance.

27. Each (state) date for Thanksgiving was different at one time.

28. This magazine (editor) idea was to make Thanksgiving a national holiday.

29. She told some of our (country) leaders of her plan.

30. Her idea had many (governors) support.

31. In 1863 Hale even got the (president) attention.

32. (Abraham Lincoln) proclamation made Thanksgiving a national holiday.

Grammar for Writing

TIP 💡
Remember, you can find out more about nouns on pages 40–55.

PROOFREADING PRACTICE

Read the text below. There are 15 mistakes in the use of nouns. Use the proofreading marks in the box to correct them.

Proofreading Marks	
∧	Add
⊙	Period
ℓ	Take out
≡	Capital letter
/	Small letter

Elm Point Elementary School is located at 246 Main Street in Smithtown. The brick building is two storys tall.

Nearly 500 boy and girls attend elm Point. Many students arrive in school bus's, but some students walk. All students enter through the buildings large blue doors. Principal Singh greets them before they go to their classroomes.

Among the students favorite places are the music and art rooms. Students take music and art class's weekly. The library is also a favorite spot. Mr. jensen, the Librarian, teaches students how to find information. A puzzle club meets there every friday.

Students play games in the gym, which also contains a stage for plays and assemblys. Just outside the gym is the playground, which has swings and a slide. There is also a rocket ship that students can climb on as they imagine an adventures in space.

Many parents who volunteer at Elm Point attended it when they were childs. They help to make Elm Point elementary School a great place for learning.

WRITE ABOUT IT

How is your school the same as Elm Point Elementary School? How is it different? Write a report that compares and contrasts the schools. Use details from the text on page 58. Include a variety of nouns in your text. Use the Writing Process Handbook on pages 236–251 to help you plan. When you are finished writing, then proofread your work.

_____

_____

_____

_____

_____

_____

_____

Check It Out! ☑

Did you . . .
- ❏ *compare and contrast your school with Elm Point Elementary School?*
- ❏ *use evidence from the text on page 58 in your response?*
- ❏ *include a variety of nouns?*
- ❏ *revise and edit your writing to show what you learned about nouns?*
- ❏ *proofread for correct spelling, capitalization, and punctuation?*

TALK ABOUT IT

Discuss: *Do all school buildings look the same? What do most school buildings have in common? How might they be different? Explain. Use a variety of nouns to talk about your ideas.*

Lesson 12: **Action Verbs**

LEARN

■ Every sentence has a subject and a predicate.
  The **verb** is the main word in the predicate.

■ Often the verb is a word that shows an action.
  An **action verb** tells what the subject does or did.

Subject	Predicate
The skier	**zooms** down the slope.
Her bright, blue skis	**flashed** in the sunlight.

PRACTICE

A Read each sentence, and look at the predicate in **boldface**.
Write the action verb in the predicate.

1. The Olympic skiers **gather at the ski slope**. _____

2. They **wear bright, colorful outfits**. _____

3. A fan **cheers for his favorite athlete**. _____

4. Many flags **wave in the breeze**. _____

5. Alpine skiers **race down steep mountain slopes**. _____

6. One skier **moves at a speed of 70 miles per hour**. _____

7. The cross-country skier **travels many kilometers**. _____

8. He **glides across the hilly landscape**. _____

9. Ski jumpers **leap long distances through the air**. _____

10. Somehow they **land on their skis**. _____

B Draw a line between the subject and the predicate of each sentence. Then write the action verb. The first one is done for you.

1. Many fans|watch the figure skaters.   *watch*

2. The skaters perform their routines well.   _____

3. One athlete traces a figure 8 on the ice.   _____

4. She spins in the air.   _____

5. The three judges score the events.   _____

6. Couples skate as pairs.   _____

7. They choose the music for these events.   _____

8. Some pairs design their own costumes.   _____

9. The male skater lifts his partner high in the air.   _____

10. The audience claps loudly.   _____

11. Ice dancers move quickly and gracefully.   _____

12. The skaters competed in a separate set of events.   _____

13. They danced to different kinds of music.   _____

14. Judges graded their artistic skills.   _____

15. The excited ice dancers waited for their scores.   _____

C *Write an action verb to complete each sentence. Choose an action verb from the box, or use an action verb of your own.*

Remember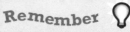
The **verb** is the main word in the predicate. The verb often shows an action.

change	cheer	covers	enter	lean
look	produces	protect	push	reach
sharpen	signals	sit	swing	wear

1. Speed skaters _____ tight, lightweight uniforms.

2. They _____ their skates before each race.

3. Some of these skaters _____ speeds of 48 kilometers per hour.

4. Helmets _____ their heads in case of falls.

5. Skating fans _____ the stadium for the big race.

6. Skaters _____ forward during the wait for the start.

7. Their eyes _____ straight ahead.

8. The official _____ the start of the race.

9. Speed skaters _____ hard on their skates with each stroke.

10. They _____ one arm back and forth.

11. A smooth flowing motion _____ the best skating rhythm.

12. The racers _____ lanes during a race.

13. Each athlete _____ the same distance that way.

14. The fans _____ on the edge of their seats.

15. They _____ the exhausted winner.

WRITE

D *Read each subject for a sentence. Write a predicate to complete the sentence. Begin each predicate with an action verb. The first one is done for you.*

1. Our town's winter sports festival _____ *begins today.* _____

2. Deep snow _____

3. The snow sculptures _____

4. Some children _____

5. A few cross-country skiers _____

6. A horse-drawn sleigh _____

7. Three speed skaters _____

8. More snow _____

9. Some workers _____

10. Two ice dancers _____

11. A brave ski jumper _____

12. A skater _____

13. A fluffy white dog _____

14. All the children _____

15. Two hockey teams _____

Proofreading Checklist ✓

❏ *Did you add a predicate to complete each sentence?*
❏ *Did you begin each predicate with an action verb?*

Lesson 13: **Present-Tense Verbs**

LEARN

- The **tense** of a verb tells when an action happens.
  The action can happen in the present, past, or future.

A verb in the **present tense** tells about an action
that happens now or happens often.

> Our uncle **drives** a fire truck.
> Fire trucks **rush** to a fire.

- A present-tense verb must *agree* with the subject
  of the sentence. The subject and the verb must
  both be singular or plural.

  - When the subject is a singular noun or *he, she,*
    or *it,* add -*s* to the verb.
    A fire **spreads** quickly in a house.
    It **leaps** from room to room.

  - When the subject is a plural noun or *I, we, you,*
    or *they,* do not add -*s* to the verb.
    Firefighters **save** lives.
    They **protect** property, too.

PRACTICE

A *Choose the verb in parentheses that agrees with the subject. Then write
the verb on the line.*

1. A loud siren _____ in the night. (wail, wails)

2. Two fire trucks _____ down our block. (roar, roars)

3. I _____ the flames in a building down the street. (spot, spots)

4. The fire captain _____ orders to the firefighters. (give, gives)

5. Two women _____ a hose to the hydrant. (connect, connects)

6. They _____ the water-filled hose at the fire. (aim, aims)

7. Other firefighters _____ the front door. (break, breaks)

8. They _____ the burning building. (enter, enters)

9. The people inside _____ to the firefighters. (shout, shouts)

10. We _____ for the best. (hope, hopes)

B *Write the present-tense form of the verb in parentheses to correctly complete each sentence.*

1. A ladder company _____ next. (arrive)

2. The firefighters _____ ladders up to the fifth floor. (raise)

3. One firefighter _____ water into the apartment. (spray)

4. She _____ yellow flames and dark smoke. (see)

5. A police officer _____ the street to traffic. (close)

6. She _____ for backup on her walkie-talkie. (call)

7. I _____ an ambulance, too. (hear)

8. The ambulance workers _____ first aid to two people. (give)

9. People _____ the building with the help of the firefighters. (leave)

10. Families _____ on the sidewalk. (stand)

11. Fire officials _____ every part of the building. (check)

12. They _____ the cause of the fire. (find)

13. The ladder company _____ all the equipment to the truck. (return)

14. All the emergency workers _____ the site at last. (leave)

15. We _____ their brave work! (appreciate)

C Ms. Wright's class wrote this list of fire-safety tips. The students made nine mistakes in subject-verb agreement. Use the proofreading marks in the box to correct the errors.

Smoke detectors save lives!

In your house each floor need a smoke detector.

Test your smoke detectors once a month. The

batteries usually lasts about one year.

Fire extinguishers puts out fires!

Small fires grow into big ones. Fire extinguishers

 stops small fires fast. Keep one in the kitchen

and another in the basement.

Fire drills keep families safe!

Many families holds fire drills at their homes. Then

each person know the safest way out during a fire.

These drills saves lives!

Careful adults hides matches!

Matches are useful, but young children plays with

them sometimes. Make sure the matches in your

house are in a safe place.

LOOK Back Did you correct nine verbs that did not agree with their subjects?

WRITE

D *Verbs show action. If you use descriptive verbs, your readers can see the action more clearly. In each sentence below, change the word in **boldface** to a more descriptive verb. Write the new sentence on the line. The first one is done for you.*

1. I **like** my uncle's work at the firehouse. _____

I admire my uncle's work at the firehouse. _____

2. Some days he **cleans** the fire truck. _____

_____

3. He **wipes** the equipment, too. _____

_____

4. A loud alarm **sounds** sometimes. _____

_____

5. "Fire!" someone **says**. _____

_____

6. The firefighters **move** toward their trucks. _____

_____

7. To get downstairs some **go** down a pole. _____

_____

8. Seconds later the trucks **travel** out the door. _____

_____

9. The fire trucks **head** to the fire. _____

_____

Go back to the sentences you wrote.
Circle the descriptive verbs you used.

Lesson 14: **More Present-Tense Verbs**

LEARN

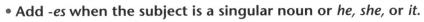

- A verb in the present tense must *agree* with the subject of the sentence. Both the subject and the verb must be either singular or plural.

- Follow these rules to make a present-tense verb agree with the subject.

For verbs that end in *ss, ch, sh, zz,* or *x*:

- **Add -*es* when the subject is a singular noun or *he, she,* or *it*.**

  press + es = press**es**   watch + es = watch**es**
  Jackie **presses** a seed into the soil.   She **watches** the seed grow.

- **Do not add -*es* when the subject is a plural noun or *I, we, you,* or *they*.**
  The students **press** seeds into the soil.
  They **watch** the seeds grow.

For verbs that end in a consonant and *y*:

- **Change *y* to *i*, and add -*es* when the subject is a singular noun or *he, she,* or *it*.**

  fly + es = fl**ies**   hurry + es = hurr**ies**
  A robin **flies** to the oak tree.   It **hurries** to its nest.

- **Do not change *y* to *i* or add -*es* when the subject is a plural noun or *I, we, you,* or *they*.**
  Robins **fly** to the oak tree.
  They **hurry** to their nests.

PRACTICE

A *Choose the verb in parentheses that agrees with the subject. Then write the verb on the line.*

1. The students _____ the signs of spring. (discuss, discusses)

2. My nose _____ from pollen in the air. (itch, itches)

3. Baby birds _____ in their nests. (hatch, hatches)

4. Geese _____ to their spring and summer homes. (fly, flies)

5. We _____ the birds in the sky. (watch, watches)

6. The air conditioner _____ on and off. (buzz, buzzes)

7. Pet owners _____ shedding hair from dogs and cats.
(brush, brushes)

8. Mom _____ the closet for lighter clothes. (search, searches)

9. Fans _____ to baseball games. (hurry, hurries)

10. The worker _____ the potholes in the road.
(patch, patches)

B *Write the present-tense form of the verb in parentheses to correctly complete each sentence.*

1. Many families _____ to do spring cleaning in April. (try)

2. Six family members _____ in old clothes. (dress)

3. Grandma _____ a broken curtain rod. (fix)

4. George _____ the windows. (wash)

5. He _____ them on a stepladder. (reach)

6. The twins _____ upstairs. (rush)

7. They _____ the wooden floors. (wax)

8. Ms. Jones _____ the garage was neater. (wish)

9. She _____ things in boxes for a garage sale. (toss)

10. Mr. Jones _____ the curtains in the sun. (dry)

11. Spring cleaning day _____ quickly. (pass)

12. The adults _____ at the end of the day. (relax)

C *Jason wrote about baseball tryouts in an email to his aunt. He made seven errors in subject-verb agreement. Use the proofreading marks in the box to correct the errors.*

I show up for the baseball tryouts every spring, and I tries my best. Baseball is my favorite sport, even though I am not the best player.

When I play left field, I miss a lot of balls. The high ones fly right over me. Fast grounders passes between my legs.

To be honest I'm not much better at the plate. The ball fly right past me, and I usually strike out. Coach Jim always stress one thing. "Don't tense up at the plate," he says. This time I relaxes. The pitcher pitch a fastball right toward me. I smack the ball hard, and it sails over the fence.

The other players rushes toward me. I get high fives from everyone. Coach Jim tells me the good news. "Congratulations! You made the team," he says. It looks like I am finally on the path to being a great athlete!

Proofreading Marks	
∧	Add
⊙	Period
ℰ	Take out
≡	Capital letter
/	Small letter

 Did you correct the seven errors in subject-verb agreement?

WRITE

The verb is the main word in the predicate of a sentence. Sometimes you can combine two related sentences by joining the verbs. Use the word *and* to join the verbs.

Charlie <u>washes</u> quickly. Charlie <u>dresses</u> quickly.
Charlie <u>washes</u> **and** <u>dresses</u> quickly.

Combining sentences in this way will make your writing smoother and clearer.

D *Combine each pair of sentences by joining the verbs.*

1. People play in the park. People relax in the park. _____

_____

2. Sue smells the cherry blossoms. Sue touches the cherry blossoms. _____

_____

3. Children make kites. Children fly kites. _____

_____

4. Karen grabs a football. Karen tosses a football. _____

_____

5. Mia sees the ball. Mia catches the ball. _____

_____

6. Their friends watch them. Their friends encourage them. _____

_____

7. Mr. Ruiz observes the players. Mr. Ruiz coaches the players. _____

_____

Go back to the sentences you wrote.
Circle the verbs that you joined.

Lesson 15: **Past-Tense Verbs**

LEARN

■ A verb in the **past tense** tells about an action that already happened.

> The students **elected** a class president.
> I **supported** one of the candidates.

■ Follow these rules to form the past tense.

- **Add -ed to most verbs.**
  help + ed = help**ed**
  All my friends **helped** Will.

- **If a verb ends in e, drop the e and add -ed.**
  vote + ed = vot**ed**
  The students **voted** on Tuesday.

- **If a verb ends in a consonant and y, change the y to i, and add -ed.**
  hurry + ed = hurr**ied**
  They **hurried** to the voting booth.

- **For most verbs that end in one vowel followed by one consonant, double the consonant, and add -ed.**
  stop + ed = **stopped**
  Our regular schoolwork **stopped** for the election.

PRACTICE

A *Write the past-tense form of each verb.*

1. study _____

2. grin _____

3. push _____

4. debate _____

5. reply _____

6. answer _____

7. decide _____

8. play _____

9. clap _____

10. carry _____

B Write the past-tense form of the verb in parentheses to correctly complete each sentence.

1. All the students _____ in the gym. (gather)

2. Our principal _____ the election rules. (explain)

3. I _____ Will for class president. (nominate)

4. Will _____ his ideas in class meetings. (express)

5. He also _____ the other candidate. (debate)

6. Both candidates _____ to the front of the room. (step)

7. Will _____ TVs in the cafeteria. (want)

8. Chris _____ possible school improvement projects. (describe)

9. Most students _____ her ideas. (like)

10. The class _____ both candidates questions. (ask)

11. I _____ a little bit about Will's chances. (worry)

12. Chris's speech _____ strong feelings. (stir)

13. We _____ a big "get out the vote" drive for Will. (plan)

14. Our teacher _____ the votes late Tuesday. (tally)

15. Everyone _____ Chris on her victory. (congratulate)

C *Chris wrote this election speech. She spelled eight past-tense verbs incorrectly. Use the proofreading marks in the box to correct the errors.*

My fellow students,

I recently finished a term as your class president, and I tryed to serve you well. I studyed the problems we faced and worked hard to make our school better. I now need another term to finish that work.

Let me briefly describe our class's successes. The first book sale we ever organized raisedd over $200. We used that money for new musical instruments.

The Everyone Can Help program grabed people's attention. More than half of our classmates applyed for volunteer jobs in the school and community.

Our talks with the cafeteria staff helpd, too. Students now have healthier meal choices, and we stoped wasting food.

A few of my campaign ideas appearedd in the newspaper. I hope you read them and will vote for me next week.

Proofreading Marks

∧	Add
⊙	Period
ℓ	Take out
≡	Capital letter
/	Small letter

Thanks for the funds!

Did you correct eight spelling mistakes with past-tense verbs?

WRITE

D *Read each pair of sentences below. In one sentence, the verb is in the past tense. In the other sentence, the verb is in the present tense. This switch in verb tense can cause confusion for the reader. Write each pair of sentences so that both verbs are in the same tense. The first one is done for you.*

1. The class president **represents** us. She **discussed** important issues with teachers.

The class president represents us. She discusses important issues with teachers.

Or: The class president represented us. She discussed important issues with teachers.

2. The vice president **helped** the president. He **attends** all the class meetings.

_____

_____

3. The class secretary **recorded** notes during meetings. He **reports** news about upcoming events, too.

_____

_____

_____

4. The treasurer **plans** fund-raisers. She **controlled** the class funds.

_____

_____

5. The student government **planned** activities for the class. It **provides** leadership.

_____

_____

_____

**Go back to each pair of sentences you wrote.
Are the verbs in the same tense?**

Lesson 16: **Future-Tense Verbs**

LEARN

- A verb in the **future tense** tells about an action that *will* happen. The action has not yet occurred. Use the special verb *will* to form the future tense.

  The Garcia family **will build** a new house.
  The builder and the Garcias **will discuss** the plans.

- The present, past, and future tenses are called **simple tenses**. They tell about action that happens now, in the past, and in the future.

  PRESENT   Ms. Garcia **studies** the plans.

  PAST   Ms. Garcia **studied** the plans.

  FUTURE   Ms. Garcia **will study** the plans.

PRACTICE

A *Read each sentence. Underline the verb. Circle **yes** if the verb is in the future tense. Circle **no** if it is not.*

1. The Garcias like the builder's plans.   *yes*   *no*

2. They will call the builder tomorrow.   *yes*   *no*

3. He will supervise the workers at the site.   *yes*   *no*

4. The builder made a schedule already.   *yes*   *no*

5. The schedule shows each part of the project.   *yes*   *no*

6. The whole project will take about three months.   *yes*   *no*

7. Many different workers will order supplies.   *yes*   *no*

8. They haul supplies in their trucks.   *yes*   *no*

9. The family will move in June.   *yes*   *no*

10. They will rent a moving truck.   *yes*   *no*

B *Complete each sentence. Write the future tense of the verb in parentheses.*

1. Carpenters _____ the frame of the house. (build)

2. They _____ each piece of lumber. (measure)

3. Then they _____ each wall separately. (construct)

4. These workers _____ the windows and doorways, too. (shape)

5. The plumbers _____ next. (arrive)

6. They _____ the kitchen and bathroom fixtures. (bring)

7. They _____ the heating system, too. (install)

8. Roofers _____ on the roof. (work)

9. They _____ shingles into place. (nail)

10. An electrician _____ a few weeks at the house. (spend)

11. She _____ wires through the house. (run)

12. She _____ the electrical system later. (test)

13. The painters _____ in early June. (start)

14. They _____ the inside and the outside of the house. (paint)

15. The Garcias _____ the colors. (choose)

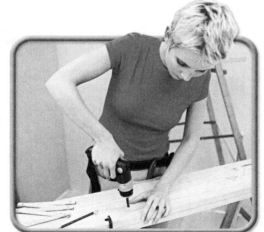

C *Daniel wrote this entry in his diary. He forgot to put seven verbs in the future tense. Use the proofreading marks in the box to correct the errors.*

Proofreading Marks

∧	Add
⊙	Period
ℒ	Take out
≡	Capital letter
/	Small letter

Dear Diary,

I can't wait until our move next Thursday! We have already packed 30 boxes with dishes, books, clothes, and toys. We probably will pack 30 more before we're done. Mom buy some new furniture for the house after we move in.

Mom and Dad rent a truck next Wednesday. It's a 24-foot truck, so everything will fit. Uncle Jack and Aunt Rita help us load it. They drive the truck over to the new house on Thursday morning. We follow them in our family car.

Once I leave here I know I will miss my old neighborhood. I miss my friends even more, but I know I come back for a visit. I also know I will make new friends at my new school.

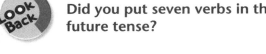

Did you put seven verbs in the future tense?

WRITE

D This builder's schedule shows the jobs that must be completed by the dates shown. On the lines below, complete the sentences about the jobs on the list. Use **will** with the verb in parentheses to form the future tense. The first one is done for you.

> **May 25** Build cabinets
> **May 26** Paint rooms
> **May 27** Install light fixtures
> **May 28** Pave driveway
> **May 29** Order kitchen appliances
>
> **June 1** Test plumbing system
> **June 2** Check roof and gutters
> **June 2–3** Plant bushes
> **June 3–4** Inspect building
> **June 3–4** Clean up job site

1. (build) The carpenter _____ *will build the cabinets.* _____

2. (paint) The painters _____

3. (install) The electrician _____

4. (pave) A paving company _____

5. (order) The builder _____

6. (test) The plumber _____

7. (check) The roofer _____

8. (plant) Landscapers _____

9. (inspect) A building inspector _____

10. (clean) The work crew _____

Proofreading Checklist

❏ *Did you write a future-tense verb in each sentence?*
❏ *Did you use **will** to form each future-tense verb?*

Lesson 17: **Linking Verbs**

LEARN

- A **linking verb** links the subject of a sentence with other words that tell about the subject. A linking verb does not show action.

    A shark **is** a meat-eating fish.
    Whale sharks **are** the largest of all sharks.

- Different forms of the verb *be* are often used as linking verbs. Use the form of *be* that agrees with the subject of the sentence.

	Forms of *be*	
Subject	**Present**	**Past**
singular noun *he, she, it*	is	was
plural noun *you, we, they*	are	were
I	am	was

The tank in this room **is** huge.
Those sharks **are** hammerheads.
I **am** curious about sharks.

It **was** open all day.
They **were** popular with visitors.
I **was** busy yesterday.

PRACTICE

A   *Read each sentence. Choose the linking verb in parentheses that agrees with the subject. Then write the linking verb on the line.*

1. We _____ at the aquarium yesterday. (was, were)

2. I _____ excited about the new shark exhibit. (was, were)

3. The tiger sharks _____ the biggest. (was, were)

4. One shark _____ 20 feet long. (was, were)

5. Shark teeth _____ razor sharp. (is, are)

6. That movie about the great white shark _____ terrifying! (was, were)

7. Some viewers _____ afraid of sharks for years. (was, were)

8. Shark attacks on humans _____ rare. (is, are)

9. The total number _____ about 100 attacks each year. (is, are)

10. About 20 attacks _____ deadly last year. (was, were)

B *Write the present-tense or past-tense form of **be** that correctly completes each sentence.*

1. The giant squid _____ one of today's rarest sea creatures.

2. Some of its tentacles _____ 90 feet long!

3. Long ago sailors _____ afraid of the giant squid.

4. To them it _____ a sea monster.

5. These days I _____ very interested in giant squids.

6. Their homes _____ far below the ocean's surface.

7. Until recently no photos of these creatures _____ available.

8. Scientists _____ unsure of the squid's size for a long time.

9. Some whales _____ enemies of the giant squid.

10. A deep, round scar on a whale _____ the mark of a squid attack.

11. The octopus _____ an ocean dweller, too.

12. It _____ a shy animal.

C *Jasmine wrote this report about piranhas. She made eight mistakes using linking verbs. Use the proofreading marks in the box to correct the errors.*

Many people is afraid of piranhas. The fear of this fish probably got started because of old movies. In old jungle movies people was often attacked by hungry piranhas.

In real life most piranhas is harmless to people. Twenty different types of piranhas live in South America. Many of them eat the fruit and nuts that fall into the water.

Red-bellied piranhas is meat eaters, though. Black piranhas are meat eaters, too. Both of these fish have sharp, pointed teeth, and their jaws is powerful. When the water level is high, these piranhas find plenty of food. They don't bother people.

During dry spells the water level falls. Then the piranhas is hungrier, and they is more dangerous. Even so, attacks on humans are rare. Of course we don't have to worry about piranhas in North America. Our climate are too cold for these fish.

Proofreading Marks

∧	Add
⊙	Period
ℰ	Take out
≡	Capital letter
/	Small letter

Did you correct eight linking verbs?

Red-bellied piranha

WRITE

D *Use a linking verb to join a subject from Box A to a word from Box B, and write a sentence. You can add other words to your sentence, and you can use a choice from a box more than once. An example is done for you.*

A

the ocean	whales
dolphins	a child

B

giants	huge
curious	mammals

1. Whales are giants of the sea. _____

2. _____

3. _____

4. _____

A

alligators	the animal
jaws	many people

B

similar	powerful
reptile	afraid

5. _____

6. _____

7. _____

8. _____

Proofreading Checklist ✓

❏ *Did you use a linking verb in each sentence?*
❏ *Did you use the correct form of the linking verb **be**?*

Lesson 18: Main Verbs and Helping Verbs

LEARN

- A verb can be more than one word. In this kind of verb, the most important word is the **main verb**. The **helping verb** usually works with the main verb to tell *when* the action happened. The helping verb always comes before the main verb.

  The moviemakers **are arriving** today.
  They **will shoot** scenes for a movie in our town.

The main verb and the helping verb form a **verb phrase**. In the verb phrases above, the main verbs are *arriving* and *shoot*. The helping verbs are *are* and *will*.

- Here are some common helping verbs.

am	was	has
is	were	have
are	will	had

- The verbs *can, may, must,* and *should* are called **modals**. These verbs are also helping verbs.

  can dance   may sing   must act   should direct

- **Conditional verbs** use *if* and helping verbs to express unlikely situations in conditional sentences. *Can, may, must, should,* and *will* are important in forming conditional sentences.

  If I watch closely, I **can learn** to make a movie.

PRACTICE

A *Read each sentence, and look at the verbs in **boldface**. Write the helping verb and the main verb on the lines.*

	Helping Verb	Main Verb
1. The movie company **has hired** a famous director.	_____	_____
2. The director **is making** an adventure film.	_____	_____
3. A chase **will occur** in the movie.	_____	_____
4. Several stunt performers **are preparing** for the scene.	_____	_____

	Helping Verb	*Main Verb*

5. If the movie set **is** ready, the director **may film** the scene today. _____ _____

6. The movie stars **should greet** their fans. _____ _____

7. People in the crowd **were cheering** for them. _____ _____

8. I **am standing** near the cameras. _____ _____

9. The director **has planned** every detail. _____ _____

10. He **had started** work on the movie months ago. _____ _____

B *Underline the verbs in each sentence. If the verb is more than one word, be sure to underline both the main verb and the helping verb. Then write the verbs on the line.*

1. If the scene is too long, the writers can make some last-minute changes. _____

2. The director had asked for the changes. _____

3. If there is a dangerous stunt, the crew tests the equipment first. _____

4. A makeup artist is applying makeup to the stars. _____

5. Electricians must check the cables before the scene is filmed. _____

6. Some stunt performers have signaled to the director. _____

7. An assistant director has requested quiet on the set. _____

8. The director shouts, "Action!" _____

9. The cameras are filming the scene. _____

10. The star jumps into a speedboat. _____

11. She has practiced this move many times. _____

12. An exciting chase scene begins. _____

C Write a helping verb and main verb to complete each sentence in this email. Choose verbs from the box, or use verbs of your own.

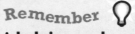

Remember

A **helping verb** works with the main verb to tell *when* an action happened.

> must walk   was explaining   has promised   are filming
>
> have watched   will appear   has scheduled   will begin

Casey,

      Something amazing has just happened! As a result, I _____ in a movie.
(1)

      As I _____ to you yesterday, some
(2)
moviemakers _____ some scenes here in
(3)
Fairport. The project is an action-adventure movie. Mom and

I _____ the filmmakers three times this week.
(4)

      Earlier today we went down to the marina to watch

again. The director saw us and asked if we wanted to

be extras in a scene. In the scene we _____
(5)
down a long dock. When we reach the middle of the

dock, a big speedboat chase _____ .
(6)

      The director _____ us for 8 o'clock
(7)
tomorrow morning. Mom _____
(8)
her that we will be there early. Look for me in

the near future at your favorite movie theater!

Write Your Own

WRITE

D *Write a sentence to answer each question. Include both a helping verb and a main verb in each of your sentences. The first one is done for you.*

1. How many movies have you watched this month? _____

I have watched three movies this month.

2. What movie have you enjoyed recently? _____

_____

3. What movie was playing last week in your community? _____

_____

4. What actors were starring in the movie? _____

_____

5. What movie is showing this week? _____

_____

6. Where is the movie playing? _____

_____

7. At about what time will this movie start? _____

_____

8. Who may join you? _____

_____

9. Which actor has created the funniest characters? _____

_____

Proofreading Checklist ☑

❏ *Did you answer each question with a complete sentence?*
❏ *Did you use a helping verb and a main verb in each sentence?*

Lesson 19: Using Helping Verbs

LEARN

- The past tense is often formed by adding -*ed* to a verb. Another way to show a past action is to use the helping verbs *has, have,* or *had* with the past-tense form of the main verb.

  Our grade **has published** a school newspaper.
  The students **have worked** hard on it.
  We **had studied** newspapers in social studies for weeks.

- Be sure to use the helping verb that agrees with the subject of the sentence.

Subject	Present	Past
singular noun *he, she, it*	has	had
plural noun *I, you, we, they*	have	had

PRACTICE

A Write **yes** or **no** to tell if the helping verb agrees with the subject of the sentence.

1. Our class has decided to publish a newspaper. _____

2. A few years ago another class had published a school newspaper. _____

3. We has learned a lot from looking at those earlier news articles and editorials. _____

4. Our staff members have selected Mike and Teresa as the head editors. _____

5. They has asked our teacher for help. _____

6. Each student have volunteered for a job. _____

7. Jon have prepared an article about our new principal, Ms. Gray. _____

8. He had interviewed her last week. _____

9. Laura had photographed the new playground. _____

10. She had borrowed her dad's digital camera for the assignment. _____

B *Draw a line under the helping verb in parentheses that correctly completes each sentence.*

1. We (has, had) named our paper *The Student News* earlier in the week.

2. Now we (has, have) renamed it *The Dover School Newsflash*.

3. Ginny (has, have) used her layout skills to design the paper.

4. She (have, had) sharpened her skills in a class last year.

5. Finally, I (has, have) finished my article about the cafeteria food.

6. Yesterday Miki (have, had) asked me to rewrite it.

7. My first draft (have, had) lacked facts and details.

8. Our teacher (has, have) suggested many story ideas to Miki.

9. She (has, have) assigned stories to writers, too.

10. Tim (has, have) roamed around the school looking for news.

11. By last week's deadline he (have, had) talked to almost everyone.

12. This week Ramon (has, have) decided to write an advice column.

13. Many classmates (has, have) handed him funny letters to answer.

14. The twins (has, have) edited most of the stories.

15. They (has, have) learned so much about grammar and punctuation.

C Sasha wrote this news story. In five of the sentences, the helping verbs **has** and **have** do not agree with the subject. Find the mistakes, and use the proofreading marks to correct them.

First-Time Racer Wins Pinewood Derby

The Pinewood Derby was held tonight in the school gym. Over two dozen participants entered the race.

Mr. Edward Ryan has held these derby races for 25 years. He have never seen a race with such fast times before.

The big winner is first-time racer Brian Little! He have finished with a best time of 3.15 seconds.

What helped Brian win? Brian says, "I has talked with some winning pinewood racers. They has given me some tips, and tips from good racers help a lot."

By coming in first Brian have earned the right to go to the regional race in Springfield next month. "I can't wait," he said. In the meantime he has started to make his car faster!

Proofreading Marks

∧	Add
⊙	Period
℘	Take out
≡	Capital letter
/	Small letter

Look Back Did you make five helping verbs agree with the subjects?

WRITE

D *Think about something exciting that happened to someone you know. Write seven sentences to tell what happened. Use past-tense verbs with the helping verbs **has, have**, or **had** in your sentences. Check a dictionary if you need help spelling a word.*

Write Your Own

1. _____

_____

2. _____

_____

3. _____

_____

4. _____

_____

5. _____

_____

6. _____

_____

7. _____

_____

Proofreading Checklist ✓

❑ *Did you use **has, have**, or **had** with the past tense verbs?*
❑ *Did you use **has** when the subject of the sentence was a singular noun or **he, she**, or **it**?*
❑ *Did you use **have** when the subject of the sentence was a plural noun or **I, you, we**, or **they**?*

Lesson 20: **Progressive Forms of Verbs**

LEARN

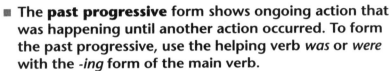

- You have learned about the present, past, and future verb tenses. Each of these tenses has a **progressive form**. The progressive form shows that an action is ongoing.

- The **present progressive** form shows ongoing action that is still happening when the words are written. To form the present progressive, use the helping verb *am*, *is*, or *are* with the *-ing* form of the main verb.

  I **am studying** about different periods in art.
  Our teacher **is explaining** how an art movement begins.
  Beth and Tom **are looking** at a painting from the Impressionist art period.

- The **past progressive** form shows ongoing action that was happening until another action occurred. To form the past progressive, use the helping verb *was* or *were* with the *-ing* form of the main verb.

  The librarian **was arranging** the books as we entered.
  We **were reading** when the books started to fall.

- The **future progressive** form shows ongoing action that will happen in the future. To form the future progressive, use the helping verb *will be* with the *-ing* form of the main verb.

  Our class **will be discussing** Impressionism this week.

- Notice the subject-verb agreement in the sentences above.

PRACTICE

A *Underline the progressive form of the verb in each sentence.*

1. We are learning about different forms of art.

2. Our art teacher was showing us different ways to hold a paintbrush when the bell rang.

3. We will be painting our own landscapes this week.

4. I am going to the pond near my house to draw.

5. Nick and Luna will be joining me at the pond tomorrow.

6. I was outlining a tree when a duck knocked over my easel.

7. My friends were laughing so hard that no one helped me pick up my painting.

8. Now Luna is sketching a picture of the duck.

9. I am thinking about painting the flowers instead of the trees.

10. Nick will be using the Impressionist style for his landscape.

B *Read each sentence. Choose the helping verb in parentheses that correctly completes the sentence. Then write the helping verb on the line.*

1. Jacob and I _____ working on a presentation on Claude Monet. (is, are)

2. Our librarian _____ gathering art books for us to examine. (is, are)

3. I _____ researching Monet's life and works of art. (am, is)

4. Jacob _____ reading about the start of the Impressionist movement. (is, were)

5. Later we _____ creating an Impressionist painting of a garden. (was, will be)

6. We _____ preparing a slideshow of Monet's paintings, too. (was, will be)

7. Jacob and I _____ giving our presentation when the fire alarm sounded. (was, were)

8. I _____ walking home when I saw a brochure for a Monet exhibit in Paris. (was, were)

9. We _____ talking about Monet's beautiful paintings when Dad came home. (is, were)

10. Now I _____ dreaming about a trip to Paris, the birthplace of Impressionism. (are, will be)

C Here is a report on the Impressionist painter Claude Monet. Write the correct present, past, or future progressive form of a verb to complete each sentence. Choose a verb from the box, or use a verb of your own.

Remember 💡
The **progressive forms** of verbs show ongoing action. To decide which helping verb to add, think about when the action began or will begin.

hope	inspire	learn	live	teach	visit

This month in art class, we _____ about the Impressionist painter Claude Monet. He is a French painter who lived from 1840 to 1926. While Monet _____ the Louvre, a museum in Paris, he saw painters copying famous masterworks, like the Mona Lisa. Unlike them, Monet drew what he saw in his own way.

Monet was not the only one in France to paint like this. Others painted this way, too. All these artists _____ in Paris at that time, and they became friends. Instead of sharp clean lines, the Impressionist painters used rapid, blurred brushstrokes. These artists developed a whole new style of art.

Monet is known for his use of color and the way he painted light. Still today, his artwork _____ artists to think in new ways. I _____ to become an artist like Monet. My dream is that one day, I _____ young artists about his work.

Proofreading Marks

∧	Add
⊙	Period
ℓ	Take out
≡	Capital letter
/	Small letter

WRITE

D *Look at the picture below. Using the progressive forms of verbs, write a story based on the picture. Include at least four different progressive forms. Use a dictionary to help with spelling.*

_____

_____

_____

_____

_____

_____

_____

_____

_____

_____

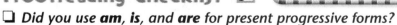

Proofreading Checklist ☑

❏ *Did you use* **am**, **is**, *and* **are** *for present progressive forms?*
❏ *Did you use* **was** *or* **were** *for past progressive forms?*
❏ *Did you use* **will be** *for future progressive forms?*

Lesson 21: **Irregular Verbs**

LEARN

- **Irregular verbs** do not add *-ed* to show the past tense. Instead, the spelling of an irregular verb changes to form the past tense. The spelling of many irregular verbs changes again when they are used with the helping verbs *has, have,* or *had.*

- There are many irregular verbs. Here are ten of them.

PRESENT   I **begin** to read Aesop's fables.

PAST   I **began** to read Aesop's fables.

PAST WITH *HAVE*   I **have begun** to read Aesop's fables.

Present	Past	Past with *has, have,* or *had*
begin	began	has, have, or had begun
bring	brought	has, have, or had brought
come	came	has, have, or had come
do	did	has, have, or had done
eat	ate	has, have, or had eaten
give	gave	has, have, or had given
grow	grew	has, have, or had grown
make	made	has, have, or had made
say	said	has, have, or had said
swim	swam	has, have, or had swum

PRACTICE

A *Write the verb in parentheses that correctly completes each sentence.*

1. A kind butcher had _____ a hungry dog some meat. (gave, given)

2. The dog _____ the meat to a bridge over a river. (bring, brought)

3. Before he _____ to eat, the dog looked down. (began, begun)

4. In the water below the bridge, another dog _____ into view. (swam, swum)

5. This dog had _____ to the river with meat, too. (came, come)

6. He stopped and slowly _____ his meat. (ate, eaten)

7. The dog on the bridge _____ greedy. (grew, grown)

8. He _____ a sudden move toward the meat reflected in the water. (make, made)

9. As soon as he had _____ that, the real meat dropped into the river. (did, done)

10. The hungry dog _____ nothing that night. (ate, eaten)

B *Write the past form of the verb in parentheses to correctly complete each sentence.*

1. A tired, hungry wolf had just _____ across a river. (swim)

2. A farmer's dog _____ barking at the wolf. (begin)

3. "I have _____ a long way," growled the wolf. (come)

4. "I have _____ nothing for days," he said. (eat)

5. The kind dog _____ the wolf some food. (bring)

6. "You must like it here," the wolf _____ . (say)

7. "The farmer has _____ a lot for me," replied the dog. (do)

8. "What has _____ that mark on your neck?" the wolf asked next. (make)

9. "I have _____ so fat that my chain is too tight," explained the dog. (grow)

10. "I would never have _____ up my freedom for a chain," the wolf said. (give)

C Evan wrote this version of an old fable called "The Fox and the Goat." He made seven mistakes with the past forms of irregular verbs. Use the proofreading marks in the box to correct the errors.

Fox had fallen into a well. He swum around for a while, but he couldn't get out.

After a while Goat came along. He had brung a bucket to get some water. "What are you doing down there, Fox?" Goat asked.

Fox looked serious. "Haven't you heard about the drought?" he asked.

Goat gived a shrug. "What drought?" he asked.

"The water shortage has growed really bad all over the country," Fox said. "In fact this may be the last water left anywhere. If I were you, Goat, I'd jump in!"

Well, the foolish goat done just that. As soon as Goat was in the well, Fox jumped on his back. Then he climbed up onto Goat's horns and out of the well.

"I'm so glad you come along," Fox called down to Goat. "You have maked my day! But next time look before you leap!"

Proofreading Marks	
∧	Add
⊙	Period
ℓ	Take out
≡	Capital letter
/	Small letter

Did you correct seven mistakes with irregular verbs?

WRITE

D *Complete the sentences in the fable below with past forms of irregular verbs. Use forms of the verbs in the chart on page 96. Then write a few sentences of your own to finish the fable. Use past forms of irregular verbs in some of your sentences.*

The ants were hard workers. All summer long they had _____ grain and vegetables in their large garden. Once fall came they _____ the food inside and stored it. They had _____ everything possible to prepare for the cold months of winter.

Grasshopper, on the other hand, _____ very little all summer and fall. When the weather was hot he _____ in the pond. When he was hungry, he _____ fresh berries off the bushes.

Winter _____ early that year, and Grasshopper _____ to worry. No berries _____ on the bushes now, and he had no food in his house. With his stomach growling, Grasshopper paid a visit to the ants.

"What has _____ you here today, Grasshopper?" asked one of the ants.

_____

_____

_____

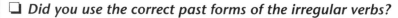

Proofreading Checklist ✓

❏ *Did you use the correct past forms of the irregular verbs?*

Lesson 22: **More Irregular Verbs**

LEARN

■ **Irregular verbs** do not form the past tense by adding -ed. Instead the spelling of an irregular verb changes when the past tense is formed. The spelling may change again when the irregular verb is used with the helping verbs *has, have,* or *had.*

PRESENT   People **write** tall tales today.

PAST   People **wrote** tall tales in the past.

PAST WITH *HAVE*   People **have written** tall tales for a long time.

Present	Past	Past with *has, have,* or *had*
break	broke	has, have, or had broken
draw	drew	has, have, or had drawn
drive	drove	has, have, or had driven
fly	flew	has, have, or had flown
ride	rode	has, have, or had ridden
sing	sang	has, have, or had sung
take	took	has, have, or had taken
tell	told	has, have, or had told
throw	threw	has, have, or had thrown
write	wrote	has, have, or had written

PRACTICE

A *Write the verb in parentheses that correctly completes each sentence.*

1. Cowboys have _____ tall tales about Pecos Bill. (tell, told)

2. They have _____ about how he was raised. (sang, sung)

3. The coyotes _____ Bill to the Texas plains. (took, taken)

4. Bill _____ faster than any other cowboy. (rode, ridden)

5. He _____ the biggest cattle to market. (drove, driven)

6. No cowboy had ever _____ a lasso so well! (threw, thrown)

7. One tale has _____ of a terrible drought. (tell, told)

8. Pecos Bill had _____ up into the sky on his horse. (rode, ridden)

9. He had _____ some storm clouds over to Texas. (drove, driven)

10. He _____ them open so the rain would fall. (broke, broken)

B *Write the past form of the verb in parentheses to correctly complete each sentence.*

1. Almost everyone _____ railroads in the early 1900s. (ride)

2. People _____ songs and tall tales about John Henry. (write)

3. Many tales have _____ about his incredible strength. (tell)

4. Henry _____ spikes into the wooden boards that hold down railroad tracks. (drive)

5. His huge sledgehammer _____ through the air. (fly)

6. Some people have _____ that Henry could swing two hammers at once! (write)

7. A folk singer _____ about Henry's contest with a new power drill. (sing)

8. Henry's boss had _____ the drill to the work site. (take)

9. The amazing contest _____ a large crowd. (draw)

10. Even after the power drill had _____, John Henry was still working. (break)

C *Sam wrote this story about Paul Bunyan, another hero of many tall tales. Sam made eight mistakes with the past forms of irregular verbs. Use the proofreading marks in the box to correct the errors.*

Proofreading Marks

∧	Add
⊙	Period
ℓ	Take out
≡	Capital letter
/	Small letter

Paul Bunyan throwed down his ax. Then he taked a deep breath. "What a job!" he said. It had took a week, but the giant logger and his big blue ox Babe were finally done. They had cleared the trees out of the Great Forests. People would now call this area the Great Plains.

"To float these logs down to my sawmill in Louisiana," Paul said, "we need a river." Paul hitched a plow to Babe and drived her and the plow down to New Orleans. Believe it or not that's how the Mississippi River got started!

"Step more lightly," Paul told Babe. Every so often her heavy hoofs breaked through the rocky ground, and streams of oil flyed up. Those were the first oil wells.

How do I know these things? Babe told me about them herself, and I have wrote down everything she said.

Did you correct eight mistakes with irregular verbs?

Write Your Own

WRITE

D The tall tale below tells what Paul Bunyan might do in today's world. Complete the sentences in the story with past forms of irregular verbs. Use forms of the verbs in the chart on page 100. Then write a few sentences of your own to complete the story. Use past forms of irregular verbs in your sentences.

Paul Bunyan and the Trees

Last year Paul Bunyan _____ across the country in a supersized truck. He _____ over other areas of the world in a jumbo jet. Along the way Paul _____ a long, hard look at the places he passed. What he saw almost _____ his heart!

Actually it was the lack of trees that almost _____ Paul crazy. "People have always _____ tall tales about my logging," he moaned. "They have even _____ songs about me and Babe working together. Maybe we have _____ this logging business too seriously. Now it's time to plant some trees!"

_____

_____

_____

_____

Proofreading Checklist ✓

❏ Did you use the correct past forms of irregular verbs?
❏ Did you use the correct form of the verb with **has, have,** and **had**?

Lesson 23: **Contractions with *Not***

LEARN

A **contraction** is made by joining two words together. An apostrophe (') takes the place of any letters that are left out. Some contractions are formed by joining a verb with the word *not*.

are + not = **aren't**
Some common beliefs about health **aren't** true.

will + not = **won't**
Carrots **won't** improve your eyesight.

Notice that the spelling of the verb *will* changes when it is combined with *not* to form the contraction *won't*.

Contractions with *not*			
is not	**isn't**	do not	**don't**
are not	**aren't**	does not	**doesn't**
was not	**wasn't**	did not	**didn't**
were not	**weren't**	cannot	**can't**
has not	**hasn't**	could not	**couldn't**
have not	**haven't**	should not	**shouldn't**
had not	**hadn't**	would not	**wouldn't**
will not	**won't**		

PRACTICE

A *Write the contraction for each pair of words.*

1. was not _____

2. cannot _____

3. does not _____

4. is not _____

5. are not _____

6. were not _____

7. did not _____

9. could not_____

8. had not _____

10. will not _____

B *Write a contraction for the word or words in parentheses to complete each sentence.*

1. Eating lots of carrots _____ turn your skin orange. (will not)

2. Worrying _____ turn a person's hair gray. (does not)

3. Too much chocolate _____ the cause of pimples. (is not)

4. Foods _____ cause all skin problems. (do not)

5. Colds _____ caused by bad weather. (are not)

6. You _____ get the flu unless you are exposed to a virus. (cannot)

7. Staying in bed _____ help you get over a cold faster. (will not)

8. Standing on your head _____ ever cured the hiccups. (has not)

9. Touching a frog _____ cause warts. (does not)

10. Scientists _____ found any evidence for this idea. (have not)

11. Everyone wishes you _____ crack your knuckles. (would not)

12. We _____ believe every health and diet tip we hear! (should not)

C *Dana and Ian wrote this fact sheet listing other untrue ideas about diet and health. In it they made eight mistakes with contractions. Use the proofreading marks in the box to correct the errors.*

Remember 💡
When you join two words in a contraction, an apostrophe takes the place of any letters that are left out.

The Truth About Diet and Health

- Drinking coffee won't stunt your growth. Even so, caffeine shouldnt be part of a young person's diet.

- Eating carrots doesnt' improve your eyesight. However the vitamin A in carrots does help eyes stay healthy.

- Going outside with wet hair wont make you catch a cold. Colds are'nt caused by wet hair or windy weather. They are caused by viruses.

- Watching TV doesnt damage your eyes. However people who spend too much time watching TV probably dont get enough exercise.

- Reading in dim light isnt a cause of bad eyesight. Good lighting, however, makes reading much easier!

- Crossing your eyes cant' make you permanently cross-eyed. But why do it? It's hard to see that way!

Proofreading Marks

∧	Add
⊙	Period
ℐ	Take out
≡	Capital letter
/	Small letter

 Did you correct eight mistakes with contractions?

WRITE

D Read each sentence. Then rewrite it using one or more contractions formed with **not**. Make any other changes that are necessary for the new sentence to make sense. The first two are done for you.

1. If you do exercise regularly, you will get in shape. _____

If you don't exercise regularly, you won't get in shape.

2. Your scrape has healed because you have taken care of it. _____

Your scrape hasn't healed because you haven't taken care of it.

3. My muscles have gotten stronger because I have exercised. _____

_____

4. If you do get eight hours of sleep, you will feel rested tomorrow. _____

_____

5. If you have eaten breakfast, you will have the energy you need. _____

_____

6. Sue did get enough vitamins because she did eat fresh fruit and vegetables. _____

_____

7. If you had acted recklessly, you would have gotten hurt. _____

_____

8. If you get caught in the rain, you will need an umbrella. _____

_____

Proofreading Checklist ☑

❏ *Did you use one or more contractions with **not** in each sentence you wrote?*

❏ *Did you use an apostrophe in place of letters that are left out?*

Unit 3 Review
Lessons 12–23

Action Verbs (pp. 60–63) *Underline the action verb in each sentence.*

1. Musicians play many different instruments in orchestras.

2. A conductor leads the orchestra.

3. Orchestras entertain people.

Present-Tense Verbs (pp. 64–71) *Write the present tense of the verb in parentheses to correctly complete each sentence.*

4. Ellen (tighten) the strings of her violin.   _____

5. The clarinet player (remove) his instrument from its case.   _____

6. The conductor (discuss) the music with the orchestra.   _____

7. Each musician (study) the music carefully.   _____

8. The ushers (guide) people to their seats.   _____

9. My sister (reach) her seat just in time.   _____

Past-Tense Verbs (pp. 72–75) *Write the past tense of the verb in parentheses to correctly complete each sentence.*

10. Early orchestras (accompany) singers.   _____

11. Composers (plan) music for more and more instruments.   _____

12. Some early orchestras (include) more than 100 musicians.   _____

Future-Tense Verbs (pp. 76–79) *Write the future tense of the verb in parentheses to correctly complete each sentence.*

13. We (go) to a concert next Friday night.   _____

14. The musicians (play) works by Mozart.   _____

15. A large crowd (attend) this performance.   _____

Linking Verbs (pp. 80–83) *Underline the linking verb that agrees with the subject of the sentence.*

16. Drums (is, are) percussion instruments.

17. Another percussion instrument (is, are) the xylophone.

18. I (am, is) a trombone player.

Main Verbs and Helping Verbs (pp. 84–91) *Underline the helping verb in each sentence.*

19. Jamie should distribute the sheet music.

20. The musicians are turning the pages.

21. The conductor will answer our questions.

Progressive Forms of Verbs (pp. 92–95) *Underline the progressive form of the verb in each sentence. Then write it on the line.*

22. Members of the orchestra are playing their scales. _____

23. Reilly and Marvin were talking about classical music. _____

24. The store will be delivering new music stands. _____

Irregular Verbs (pp. 96–103) *Underline the correct verb in parentheses to complete each sentence.*

25. Our orchestra (began, begun) today's practice at two o'clock.

26. All the members have (took, taken) their seats.

27. Jesse had (wrote, written) one of the songs we will perform.

Contractions with *Not* (pp. 104–107) *Read each sentence. Write the words in **boldface** as a contraction.*

28. Some of the instruments **are not** in tune. _____

29. We **do not** get discouraged. _____

30. Our performance **will not** be perfect until we practice more. _____

TIP 💡
Remember, you can find out more about verbs and contractions on pages 60–107.

PROOFREADING PRACTICE

Read the text below. There are 15 mistakes in the use of verb tenses and contractions. Use the proofreading marks in the box to correct them.

Proofreading Marks	
∧	Add
⊙	Period
ℓ	Take out
≡	Capital letter
/	Small letter

Sometimes I wonder what life was like for children in the past. What was American children doing 300 years ago?

Children in Colonial America works hard. Most families back then lived on farms, so boys got up at sunrise and do farm chores. Girls have home chores; they would sew, knit, and cooked. Both boys and girls milked cows, feeded hens, and fetched water. Colonial children sometimes played, too. They liked hopscotch and tag; they flyed kites and runned races.

Most towns lacked schools, so many children didnt have the opportunity to go to school. If a town had a school, boys might attend, but girls often stays home. I dont' think that was fair.

At mealtimes, family members sat on benches if they has them, but they often ate standing up. They picking up food with spoons or with just their hands. The whole family shared a little house with one or two rooms, and everybody sleeped in straw beds. I wouldnt like that because I would be waking up all night long!

WRITE ABOUT IT

If you had lived in colonial times, what might your life have been like? Write a description. Use details from the text on page 110. Include a variety of verb tenses and contractions in your description. Use the Writing Process Handbook on pages 236–251 to help you plan. When you are finished writing your draft, then proofread your work.

Check It Out! ☑

Did you . . .
- ❏ **describe what your life might have been like in colonial times?**
- ❏ **use evidence from the text on page 110 in your response?**
- ❏ **write a topic sentence that tells your main idea?**
- ❏ **include sentences with supporting details?**
- ❏ **revise and edit your writing to show what you learned about verbs?**
- ❏ **proofread for correct spelling, capitalization, and punctuation?**

TALK ABOUT IT

Discuss: *Was it fair that children in colonial times often did not have opportunities to attend school? Why or why not? Explain. Use a variety of verb tenses and contractions to talk about your ideas.*

Lesson 24: **Adjectives**

LEARN

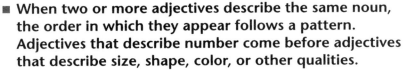

- An **adjective** is a word that describes a noun. It can tell *what kind*, and it can also tell *how many*. An adjective usually comes before the noun it describes.

WHAT KIND	We visited a **large** refuge.
HOW MANY	**Several** birds live in the refuge.

- When two or more adjectives describe the same noun, the order in which they appear follows a pattern. Adjectives that describe number come before adjectives that describe size, shape, color, or other qualities.

  Two white swans have built a nest there.
  They used **many dry** twigs to make the nest.

- An adjective can also come after the noun it describes. This usually happens when the adjective follows a form of the verb *be*.

  The swan's nest is **round**.
  The eggs are **white**.

PRACTICE

A *Circle the adjective(s) that describe the noun in **boldface**.
Then write the adjective(s) on the line.*

1. A patient **swan** sits on the nest.   _____

2. She protects three small **eggs**.   _____

3. The nest is near a beautiful **lake**.   _____

4. The swan chose a safe **location** for the nest.   _____

5. Tall **grass** surrounds the nest.   _____

6. Few **enemies** bother the birds here.   _____

7. The **eggs** are large. _____

8. The babies have sharp **beaks**. _____

9. Their beaks break the hard **eggshells**. _____

10. Soon the **babies** are free. _____

B *Circle the adjective(s) in each sentence, and underline the noun they describe. Then write the adjective(s) on the line.*

1. Several ducks live near the lake. _____

2. Their feathers are waterproof. _____

3. Their feet are webbed. _____

4. Many hungry ducks dive for food. _____

5. They eat insects and small plants. _____

6. Their grassy nests are on the shore. _____

7. The geese near the lake are noisy. _____

8. Their honking is loud! _____

9. Five babies may follow an adult. _____

10. Their feathers are fluffy. _____

11. Nine geese are flying in a pattern. _____

12. The pattern is v-shaped. _____

13. The geese are watchful. _____

14. A goose is fierce at times. _____

15. Even the babies are bold! _____

C *Write an adjective to complete each sentence. Choose an adjective from the box, or use an adjective of your own.*

Remember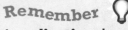
An **adjective** describes a noun.
It can tell *what kind* or *how many*.

beautiful	brown	clear	cute	flat
gentle	green	happy	long	peaceful
sandy	short	soft	sunny	tall

1. We went to the bird refuge on a _____ day.

2. The sky above was _____.

3. A _____ breeze rippled the water.

4. A _____ heron waded along the shore.

5. Its legs were _____.

6. _____ water lilies were blooming on the lake.

7. A _____ frog sat on a lily pad.

8. Its _____ croak faded into silence.

9. Seven _____ ducklings were swimming with their mother.

10. We walked down a _____ path along the pond.

11. A snake slept on a _____ rock.

12. Three _____ hawks circled overhead.

13. The _____ buzzing of insects filled the air.

14. The bird refuge is so _____.

15. I was _____ to be there.

Combining Sentences

WRITE

Sometimes you can combine two related sentences into one sentence by moving an adjective.

In the example below only the second sentence has an adjective. To make one smooth sentence, you can place the adjective *noisy* before the noun *blue jay* in the first sentence.

A blue jay squawked at a squirrel. The blue jay was <u>noisy</u>.
A <u>noisy</u> blue jay squawked at a squirrel.

In this example both sentences have adjectives. You can combine the sentences by placing the adjective *big* in the second sentence after the adjective *seven* in the first sentence.

<u>Seven</u> turkeys hurried by. The turkeys were big.
<u>Seven</u> <u>big</u> turkeys hurried by.

D *The sentences in each pair below are related. Move the adjective from one sentence to the other to combine the sentences. Write the new sentence on the line.*

1. Two doves rested on a branch. The doves were gray. _____

_____

2. A hawk's shadow passed over the lake. It was a dark shadow. _____

_____

3. A raven's call broke the silence. It was a harsh call. _____

_____

4. The sound echoed across the lake. The sound was mysterious. _____

_____

5. We saw different kinds of birds. We saw eight different kinds. _____

_____

Go back to the sentences you wrote.
Circle the adjective or adjectives.

Lesson 25: *A, An, The*

LEARN

■ The special adjectives *a*, *an*, and *the* are called **articles**. These small words come before nouns.

    a raccoon   **an** otter   **the** animals

■ The articles *a* and *an* refer to any person, place, or thing. The article *the* refers to a specific person, place, or thing.

    An elephant can run faster than **a** person.
    The runner crossed **the** finish line at noon.

- Use *a* before a singular noun that begins with a consonant sound.

    I found **a** book of interesting facts.

- Use *an* before a singular noun that begins with a vowel sound.

    Each fact described **an** animal.

- Use *the* before both singular and plural nouns.
    The facts about **the** insect surprised me.

PRACTICE

A   *Some sentences have more than one article. Circle each article, and write it on the line. The first one is done for you.*

1. It is impossible for ⟨a⟩ pig to look up into ⟨the⟩ sky.   _____*a, the*_____

2. A sleeping bear in winter can go 100 days without water.   _____

3. An ostrich never buries its head in the sand.   _____

4. There are more than 20 muscles in the ear of a cat.   _____

5. An insect buzzes because of the movement of its wings.   _____

6. A cockroach can run one meter per second.   _____

7. The pattern of a zebra's black-and-white stripes is formed by its hair.   _____

8. A snail can sleep for three years. _____

9. Wolves don't howl more often when the moon is full. _____

10. A shark's mouth has six to twenty rows of teeth. _____

B *Write the article in parentheses that correctly completes each sentence.*

1. _____ elephant flaps its ears to stay cool. (A, An)

2. The Chow Chow is _____ dog with a blue tongue. (a, the)

3. Some spiders can spin _____ web in 30 minutes. (a, an)

4. A koala is not _____ bear. (a, the)

5. It is _____ relative of the kangaroo. (a, an)

6. Females carry their young in _____ pouch. (a, an)

7. A zorilla is _____ animal that looks like a skunk. (a, an)

Zorilla

8. Zorillas, like skunks, use odor as _____ defense. (a, an)

9. The American buffalo is not _____ buffalo at all. (a, the)

10. It is _____ bison. (a, an)

11. An Andean condor can have _____ wingspan of 10 feet. (a, an)

12. It is one of the largest flying birds in _____ world. (a, the)

13. The world's smallest mammal is _____ bat. (a, an)

14. This tiny bat is the size of _____ bumblebee. (a, an)

15. _____ ostrich is a bird that does not fly. (A, An)

C *Sean wrote a report about how certain animals communicate their emotions. In this part of the report, he used five articles incorrectly. Use the proofreading marks in the box to correct the errors.*

Does a animal have emotions? That's not easy to answer. How could we tell if animals did feel the emotion? After all they can't talk. Sometimes, however, animals do express feelings through body language.

For example, if the dog has misbehaved, it might turn its head sideways and show its neck. It might also crouch down and lift its front paw to show you it is sorry. Wolves, which are wild relatives of dogs, might also show these two types of body language.

Wolves live in the pack with one strong leader. Pack members use body language to show that they recognize their leader. To your dog you are a leader of the pack, so it uses the same kind of body language with you.

Proofreading Marks

∧	Add
⊙	Period
℘	Take out
☰	Capital letter
/	Small letter

Did you correct five mistakes with articles?

WRITE

D Write a sentence about each animal below. In each sentence use an article before the animal's name, and use the information given in parentheses. After writing your sentence go back and add an adjective to each sentence. The first one is done for you.

1. blue whale (weighs up to 200 tons)

A blue whale weighs up to 200 tons.

A big blue whale weighs up to 200 tons.

2. butterfly (flaps its wings five times per second)

_____

_____

3. humpback whale (can eat one ton of food per day)

_____

_____

4. opossum (sleeps 19 hours per day)

_____

_____

5. hummingbird (can fly backward)

_____

_____

Go back to the sentences you wrote.
Circle each article you used.
Underline each adjective you added.

Lesson 26: **Demonstrative Adjectives**

LEARN

■ Adjectives can tell *what kind* or *how many*. Adjectives can also tell *which one*. Adjectives that tell *which one* are called **demonstrative adjectives**.

This, that, these, and *those* are demonstrative adjectives. Use *this* and *that* before singular nouns. Use *these* and *those* before plural nouns.

This film is very popular.
That book is a favorite of young children.
These children are here for Story Time.
Those adults are waiting for them.

■ *This* and *these* refer to people, places, or things that are nearby. Do not use *here* after *this* or *these*.

CORRECT	The children's librarian has chosen **this book**.
INCORRECT	The children's librarian has chosen **this here book**.
CORRECT	**These children** want to hold the book.
INCORRECT	**These here children** want to hold the book.

■ *That* and *those* refer to people, places, or things that are farther away. Do not use *there* after *that* or *those*.

CORRECT	Everyone will sit in **that room**.
INCORRECT	Everyone will sit in **that there room**.
CORRECT	**Those children** want to hear the story again.
INCORRECT	**Those there children** want to hear the story again.

PRACTICE

A *Underline the demonstrative adjective in each sentence. Then write it on the line.*

1. The new library is on this block.   _____

2. It used to be in that old building.   _____

3. Let's use those computers to search the online catalog.   _____

4. These books are novels by Laura Ingalls Wilder. _____

5. Ask that librarian if you need help to find a book. _____

6. These picture books belong in the children's section. _____

7. Those volunteers will sort the books by author. _____

8. This room is the Listening Room. _____

9. Use these earphones to listen to music. _____

10. Let's make a reservation to use this equipment again. _____

B *Write the demonstrative adjective in parentheses that correctly completes each sentence.*

1. Look at the picture in _____ book about New York City. (this, these)

2. It shows _____ building across the street. (this, that)

3. _____ famous structure is the 42nd Street Library. (That, Those)

4. The library was built on _____ two blocks over there. (this, those)

5. Look at _____ marble lions at the library entrance. (that, those)

6. _____ big cat next to me is nicknamed Patience. (This, That)

7. _____ big cat on the other side is nicknamed Fortitude. (This, That)

8. Let's go up _____ stone steps and into the main entrance. (this, these)

9. _____ magnificent library has eleven reading rooms. (This, Those)

10. Readers can find some useful books in _____ reading areas. (this, these)

11. There are 42 oak tables in _____ huge room. (that, these)

12. Up to 16 people can sit at each of _____ oak tables. (this, those)

C Angie wrote this script for a tour of the new town library. She made six mistakes when using demonstrative adjectives. Use the proofreading marks in the box to correct the errors.

Proofreading Marks

∧	Add
⊙	Period
ℒ	Take out
≡	Capital letter
/	Small letter

Welcome to our new library! We'll begin our tour in the reference section. These here books all around us are reference books. You'll find dictionaries, encyclopedias, and atlases on the shelves. This woman standing over there is Ms. Charles. She is our reference librarian.

In that corner over there, we see the periodical room. Newspapers and magazines are called periodicals. Everyone can go there to read those there magazines and papers.

The library is a great place to do research. These computers against the far wall are for everyone to use. That sheet of paper in my hand lists the rules for computer use.

Finally, here we are in the media section. For many people that is their favorite part of the library. Audiobooks, videos, eReaders, and eBooks are available. You can borrow them just like books!

Look Back Did you correct six mistakes with demonstrative adjectives?

WRITE

D *Imagine you are giving a tour of your classroom from where you sit. Start by listing two things or areas of the classroom that are near you. Then list two things or areas of the classroom that are farther away. A sample is done for you.*

Near	*Farther Away*
the library corner	

Now write a sentence with a demonstrative adjective that tells something about the things or areas of the classroom you have listed. You can use the sample below as a model.

1. This area on the left is the library corner. We have books on many

subjects on these shelves.

2.

3.

4.

Proofreading Checklist ✔

❏ *Did you use **this** and **these** to refer to things that are nearby?*

❏ *Did you use **that** and **those** to refer to things that are farther away?*

Lesson 27: **Comparing with Adjectives**

LEARN

■ **Adjectives can compare people, places, and things. Adjectives that compare tell how things are different from each other.**

Lions are **stronger** than leopards.
Lions are the **strongest** big cat.

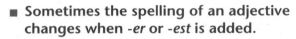

- **Add -*er* to most adjectives to compare two people, places, or things.**
  strong + er = strong**er**

- **Add -*est* to most adjectives to compare more than two people, places, or things.**
  strong + est = strong**est**

■ **Sometimes the spelling of an adjective changes when -*er* or -*est* is added.**

- **If an adjective ends in *e*, drop the *e* and add -*er* or -*est*.**
  large + er = larg**er**   large + est = larg**est**

- **If an adjective ends in a consonant and *y*, change the *y* to *i* and add -*er* or -*est*.**
  hungry + er = hungr**ier**   hungry + est = hungr**iest**

- **If an adjective ends in one vowel followed by a consonant, double the consonant and add -*er* or -*est*.**
  big + er = big**ger**   big + est = big**gest**

PRACTICE

  *In Column A add -**er** to each adjective. In Column B add -**est** to each adjective. Remember to make the necessary spelling changes before adding -**er** and -**est**.*

	A		*B*
1. cold	_____	**6.** warm	_____
2. wild	_____	**7.** simple	_____
3. scarce	_____	**8.** late	_____
4. tiny	_____	**9.** shady	_____
5. hot	_____	**10.** thin	_____

B *Write the form of the adjective in parentheses that correctly completes each sentence.*

1. Lions are the _____ members of the cat family. (large)

2. Lions are _____ than humans. (strong)

3. They can drag _____ weights than people can. (heavy)

4. They are _____ than any other cat. (mighty)

5. Lions are not the _____ of the big cats. (fast)

6. They are usually _____ than their prey. (slow)

7. A zebra, for example, is _____ than a lion. (swift)

8. Vision is the _____ of a lion's five senses. (sharp)

9. A lion can see in _____ light than you can. (dim)

10. A lion's night vision is _____ than its prey's night vision. (keen)

11. Hunting at night is _____ than hunting during the day. (easy)

12. A female lion is _____ than a male lion. (small)

13. Females are _____ hunters than males. (fierce)

14. Of all the cats, lions have the _____ roar. (loud)

15. Many people think that lions are the _____ animals of all. (grand)

C *Lena wrote this report about tigers. She made seven mistakes when using and spelling adjectives that compare. Use the proofreading marks in the box to correct the errors.*

Tigers are an endangered animal. Three kinds of tigers have become extinct. Six other kinds survive. Of these six groups, the larger are the Siberian tigers.

About 400 Siberian tigers are found in Asia. A biger population lives in eastern Russia. These big cats survive in some of the icyest forests on Earth.

Most Bengal tigers live in India, but a smallest population is found in Nepal. Bengal tigers tend to live in the hotest and wettest regions of India.

Indochinese tigers live mainly in the jungles of Thailand. There may be fewwer than 1500 left.

Sumatran tigers are a fourth type of tiger. About 400 of them live on the island of Sumatra. Of all the types, these have the darker coats.

Finally, there are the Malaysian tiger and the South China tiger, the rarest kind. None may be left in China.

Proofreading Marks

∧	Add
⊙	Period
ℒ	Take out
≡	Capital letter
/	Small letter

Did you correct seven adjectives that compare?

126 ■ Unit 4

WRITE

D *Follow the directions below to write groups of three sentences. In your first sentence use the adjective in parentheses. In your second sentence use the adjective with **-er**. In your third sentence use the adjective with **-est**. The first one is done for you.*

1. Use the following information about weight to compare these three big cats. (heavy)

Cheetah 160 pounds   **Lion** 400 pounds   **Siberian tiger** 700 pounds

A cheetah is heavy.

A lion is heavier than a cheetah.

The Siberian tiger is the heaviest of the three cats.

2. Use the following information about top speeds to compare these three cats. (fast)

Leopard 36 mph   **Lion** 50 mph   **Cheetah** 70 mph

_____

_____

_____

3. Use the following information about body length (including the tail) to compare these three big cats. (long)

Leopard 6 feet   **Cheetah** 7 feet   **Lion** 9 feet

_____

_____

_____

Proofreading Checklist ☑

❑ *Did you use an adjective with -er to compare two of the big cats?*

❑ *Did you use an adjective with -est to compare the three big cats?*

Lesson 28: **Comparing with *More* and *Most***

LEARN

The words *more* and *most* are often needed when comparing adjectives of two or more syllables.

- Use *more* with adjectives when comparing two people, places, or things.

    Football is **more popular** than soccer in the United States.

- Use *most* with adjectives when comparing more than two people, places, or things.

    Soccer is the **most popular** sport in the world.

- Do not add *-er* or *-est* to an adjective when you use *more* or *most* to compare.

CORRECT	Jean is **more patient** than Debbie.
INCORRECT	Jean is **more patienter** than Debbie.
CORRECT	Carlos has the **most awesome** kick.
INCORRECT	Carlos has the **most awesomest** kick.

PRACTICE

A *Change each adjective in Column A to compare two. Change each adjective in Column B to compare more than two. Write the new adjectives on the lines.*

	A		*B*
1. honest	_____	**6.** generous	_____
2. active	_____	**7.** loyal	_____
3. complex	_____	**8.** difficult	_____
4. responsible	_____	**9.** basic	_____
5. famous	_____	**10.** independent	_____

B *Complete each sentence. Add **more** or **most** to the adjective in parentheses. Write the words on the line.*

1. Why is soccer the _____ game in the world? (popular)

2. Many fans claim soccer is _____ than baseball. (exciting)

3. According to them it is also _____ than football. (enjoyable)

4. Soccer is the _____ game I have ever played. (active)

5. In football breaks in the action are _____ than in soccer. (frequent)

6. Nonstop action is soccer's _____ feature. (appealing)

7. Other sports have _____ rules than soccer. (complicated)

8. The rules for football are probably the _____ of all. (complex)

9. As a result football is _____ to learn than soccer. (challenging)

10. Soccer also has the _____ equipment of any team sport. (basic)

11. That helps make it the _____ sport of all. (affordable)

12. Baseball equipment is _____ than soccer equipment. (expensive)

13. Setting up a football field is _____ than setting up a soccer field. (demanding)

14. Soccer fans may be the _____ sports fans in the world. (spirited)

15. They may also be the _____ fans in the world. (loyal)

C Eric wrote this journal entry about playing soccer. He made six mistakes when he used adjectives to compare. Use the proofreading marks in the box to correct the errors.

Everyone wants to win at soccer. Winning, however, is not my most importantest goal. Learning teamwork, playing fairly, and having fun are my main reasons for playing. To me, being in top shape is a more importanter goal than being on the top team.

Of the dozens of soccer leagues in the state, ours has the best teams. We play against the most skillfullest athletes in our age group. Win or lose, I enjoy the competition. And when the season is over, I know I've improved. My passes are most accurate than before, and I understand the game a little better.

Now that the season is about to start, I am looking forward to the more exciting year the team has ever had. Even though I play mainly for the love of the game, I also hope it is the more successful season ever!

Proofreading Marks	
∧	Add
⊙	Period
ꝰ	Take out
≡	Capital letter
/	Small letter

Did you correct six mistakes in adjectives that compare?

WRITE

D Write three sentences to compare the three sports in each group. In your first sentence, use the adjective in parentheses. In your second sentence, use **more** with the adjective. In your third sentence, use **most** with the adjective. The first one is done for you.

1. tennis   baseball   golf   (exciting)

Golf is exciting to watch.

Tennis is more exciting than golf.

Baseball is the most exciting of the three sports.

2. kickball   dodgeball   softball   (enjoyable)

_____

_____

_____

3. basketball   hockey   football   (challenging)

_____

_____

_____

4. diving   figure skating   swimming   (graceful)

_____

_____

_____

Proofreading Checklist ☑

❏ *Did you use **more** with an adjective to compare two sports?*
❏ *Did you use **most** with an adjective to compare three sports?*

Lesson 29: **Comparing with** *Good* **and** *Bad*

LEARN

■ The adjectives *good* and *bad* have special forms for comparing.

Adjective	Compare Two	Compare More Than Two
good	better	best
bad	worse	worst

- Use *better* when comparing two people, places, or things. Use *best* when comparing more than two.

    A dog makes a **good** pet.
    A cat makes a **better** pet than a dog.
    A parrot makes the **best** pet of all.

- Use *worse* when comparing two people, places, or things. Use *worst* when comparing more than two.

    The rain brought **bad** weather.
    The sleet brought **worse** weather.
    The ice storm brought the **worst** weather of all.

PRACTICE

A *Underline the form of **good** or **bad** in each sentence. Then write the word on the line.*

1. Walking my dog, Lucky, is the best way for me to exercise. _____

2. Walking Lucky is better than playing softball. _____

3. Lucky and I took the worst shortcut to the park. _____

4. The path was worse than the road we always take. _____

5. It was the worst idea I ever had. _____

*Write the form of **good** or **bad** in parentheses that correctly completes each sentence.*

6. Our pet rabbit did the _____ thing yesterday. (worse, worst)

7. Was it _____ than what he did last week? (worse, worst)

8. Eating flowers in the garden was the _____ thing he ever did. (worse, worst)

9. We must put a _____ fence around the flower bed. (better, best)

10. The _____ kind of fence is one with no openings. (good, best)

B *Write the form of the adjective in parentheses that correctly completes each sentence.*

1. The forest is the _____ place to see woodland animals. (good)

2. Morning is a _____ time of day to see a deer. (good)

3. A hot afternoon is the _____ time. (bad)

4. Did you know that some flowers have a _____ smell? (bad)

5. The _____ ones of all smell like rotting meat. (bad)

6. This _____ odor attracts flies. (bad)

7. Is the odor _____ than the odor of a skunk? (bad)

8. Look up to get an even _____ view of the birds. (good)

9. This trail leads to the _____ spot for bird watching. (good)

10. It is a _____ trail than the rocky one. (good)

11. This picture of the rabbit is _____ than the first one. (bad)

12. Still it is _____ than the picture of the woodpecker. (good)

C Martin wrote this report about a class trip. He made six mistakes using the different forms of **good** and **bad**. Use the proofreading marks in the box to correct the errors.

Last week, our class visited the new aquarium. It has the better exhibit of ocean life I've ever seen.

During our visit, we had the best tour ever. First, our tour guide took us to see a film about rare and dangerous animals. Then she took us to see something even best than the tour. She led us to a circular fish tank that had a spiral ramp wrapped around it. The tank was four floors high and filled with a variety of fish, sharks, and sea turtles. It was awesome! Unfortunately, I was standing next to a baby carriage. The baby inside was crying really loudly. It was the worse spot of all to be standing. Then I saw that Paula's spot was worst than mine. She was standing behind a man who was 6 feet tall!

I really enjoyed this class trip. The better part was watching a diver feed the animals in the tank. The worse part was having to leave the aquarium.

Proofreading Marks

∧	Add
⊙	Period
ꞁ	Take out
≡	Capital letter
/	Small letter

Did you correct six forms of *good* and *bad*?

WRITE

Additional Resources at
SadlierConnect.com

D *Write about a trip you took with your class.*
Tell where you went and what you saw.
Describe the best part and worst part of the trip.
*Include the words **better**, **best**, **worse**, and **worst***
in your descriptions. Check a dictionary if you need
help spelling a word.

_____

_____

_____

_____

_____

_____

_____

_____

_____

_____

_____

_____

_____

_____

_____

_____

Proofreading Checklist ☑

❏ *Did you use **better** and **worse** to compare two people,*
places, or things?
❏ *Did you use **best** and **worst** to compare more than two?*

Lesson 30: **Adverbs**

LEARN

■ An **adverb** is a word that generally describes a verb. Adverbs describe verbs by telling *how, when,* or *where* an action happens. Many adverbs end in *-ly.*

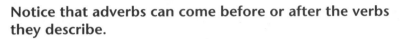

HOW	The news reporters work **hard**. They check the facts **carefully**.
WHEN	The evening news will begin **soon**. The team **always** prepares in advance.
WHERE	The news van rushes **ahead**.

Notice that adverbs can come before or after the verbs they describe.

■ Here are some adverbs that tell *how.*

slowly	suddenly	quietly	well	badly
fast	together	hard	easily	quickly

■ Here are some adverbs that tell *when.*

yesterday	often	always	then	usually
next	tomorrow	later	soon	recently

■ Here are some adverbs that tell *where.*

here	there	outside	below	near
upstairs	locally	everywhere	ahead	far

PRACTICE

A *Circle the adverb that describes the verb in **boldface**. Write whether the adverb tells **how, when,** or **where**.*

1. Aunt Sonia always **wanted** to be a reporter. _____

2. She recently **got** her wish. _____

3. Today, she **is** a reporter at a TV news studio. _____

4. Many other reporters **work** there with her. _____

5. The news director **plans** the assignments carefully. _____

PRACTICE **A** *continued*

6. Aunt Sonia often **interviews** people.   _____

7. She **tries** hard to ask good questions.   _____

8. She **travels** everywhere for stories.   _____

9. A camera crew usually **follows** her.   _____

10. Later, she **writes** the news story.   _____

B *Circle the adverb in each sentence, and underline the verb that it describes. Then write the adverb on the line.*

1. Aunt Sonia visited city hall recently.   _____

2. Her news crew went there to cover the city spelling bee.   _____

3. Over 100 students usually enter the event.   _____

4. I gladly participated in the spelling bee.   _____

5. I was always a good speller.   _____

6. I bravely attempted each spelling.   _____

7. I spelled many words correctly.   _____

8. My aunt smiled happily.   _____

9. One student finally won the bee.   _____

10. Everyone clapped wildly for the winner.   _____

11. Aunt Sonia interviewed the winner afterwards.   _____

12. Then she interviewed some other students.   _____

13. The camera crew filmed steadily.   _____

14. I looked directly into the camera.   _____

15. Watch for me tonight on the news.   _____

C *Write an adverb to complete each sentence. Choose an adverb from the box, or use an adverb of your own. The clue in parentheses will help you. The first one is done for you.*

 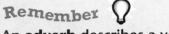
> clearly   fairly   far   locally   next   usually

1. News reporters must describe events _____*clearly*_____ . (how)

2. They must also present stories _____ . (how)

3. Facts are _____ double-checked at the studio. (when)

4. News editors decide which stories to cover _____ . (when)

5. Reporters might investigate stories _____ or nationally. (where)

6. They might travel near or _____ for a story. (where)

> always   anywhere   correctly   quickly   sometimes   well

7. News video can take viewers _____ . (where)

8. The video should work _____ with the story. (how)

9. A news anchorperson _____ reads the news. (when)

10. A good anchor reads each story _____ . (how)

11. The anchor _____ interviews people on air. (when)

12. Thanks to the news broadcast, we _____ learn what is happening. (how)

WRITE

D *Adverbs make sentences clearer and more interesting. Read these sentences from a news report about a snowstorm. Then rewrite each one, adding an adverb. Your adverb should tell how, when, or where an action happens. The first one is done for you.*

1. The worst snowstorm in 40 years hit Riverview. _____

The worst snowstorm in 40 years hit Riverview (yesterday).

2. The snow fell for over 24 hours. _____

_____

3. Snowplows are working to clear the streets. _____

_____

4. All city schools will close. _____

_____

5. City officials are checking weather reports. _____

_____

6. More snow and strong winds will arrive. _____

_____

7. Also, temperatures are falling. _____

_____

8. We can't expect any relief! _____

_____

Go back to the sentences you wrote.
Circle the adverbs that you added.

Lesson 31: **Comparing with Adverbs**

LEARN

■ An **adverb** can compare two or more actions.

- Add *-er* to most one-syllable adverbs to compare two actions.
  Jason runs **faster** than I do.

- Add *-est* to most one-syllable adverbs to compare more than two actions.
  Tran runs **fastest** of all the students in our class.

■ The words *more* and *most* can also be used with adverbs to compare. Use *more* and *most* with most adverbs that have two or more syllables, including adverbs that end in *-ly*.

- Use *more* with adverbs to compare two actions.
  Ian leaps **more gracefully** than Tai.

- Use *most* with adverbs to compare more than two actions.
  Of all the athletes in our school, Megan leaps **most gracefully**.

- Do not add *-er* or *-est* to an adverb when you use *more* or *most*.

PRACTICE

A Write the adverb in parentheses that correctly completes each sentence.

1. Our track club practices _____ in spring than in winter. (harder, hardest)

2. Saturday is the day we begin _____. (earlier, earliest)

3. Today, I jogged _____ than I did yesterday. (longer, longest)

4. Beginners should run _____ than experienced runners. (more slowly, most slowly)

5. Of all the members in our club, Sonia can jump _____. (higher, highest)

6. Runners must breathe _____ than walkers. (more deeply, most deeply)

7. I run _____ on grass than on the sidewalk. (more comfortably, most comfortably)

8. Of all the club runners, Alex practices _____. (more frequently, most frequently)

9. Of the three clubs, ours trains _____ for the 5-kilometer race. (more seriously, most seriously)

10. We have competed _____ than we did last year. (more successfully, most successfully)

B *Write the form of the adverb in parentheses that correctly completes each sentence.*

1. Of the eight runners in the 100-meter race, Alberto ran

_____. (fast)

2. I sprinted _____ than Neil did. (quickly)

3. The high jump took _____ to organize than the 5-kilometer race. (long)

4. I've practiced _____ this year than last year. (hard)

5. Fans cheered _____ for the long jump than for the 5-kilometer race. (loud)

6. Of all the races, I cheered _____ for the relay. (wildly)

7. In the long jump, Nilda jumped _____ than Rachel. (confidently)

8. Of the many sprinters, Lin ran _____. (rapidly)

9. She certainly ran _____ than I did. (smoothly)

10. I hope our team performs _____ than any other team. (impressively)

C Jenna wrote this story for the sports section of her school newspaper. She made six mistakes when using adverbs that compare. Use the proofreading marks in the box to correct the errors.

> The Track and Field Festival at Town Park on April 1 was a big success. Of the three track clubs, the Lions performed more successfully. "All the athletes performed more skillfully than last year," Coach Chen said.
>
> Over twelve runners took part in the 5-kilometer race. Jan Ruiz ran most fastest. As usual, she also ran the most gracefully of all the athletes.
>
> Tom Powers took first prize in the high jump, jumping more higher than he did in his record jump. Of the many athletes in the long jump, Carla Allen jumped farther.
>
> All three clubs had teams in the relay race. The Aces ran fastest. They also handed off the baton more smoothlier than the Trackers.
>
> A large crowd gathered, and people cheered more loudlier as the day went on. All in all, the future of track in this town looks bright!

Proofreading Marks

∧	Add
⊙	Period
ℰ	Take out
≡	Capital letter
/	Small letter

Did you correct six mistakes in adverbs that compare?

WRITE

D *Write two sentences to describe what is happening in each picture. Use the adverbs in parentheses to compare the actions of the athletes.*

1. (fast) _____

_____

2. (gracefully) _____

_____

3. (high) _____

_____

4. (impressively) _____

_____

Proofreading Checklist ✓

❏ *Did you add* **-er** *or* **–est** *to the one-syllable adverbs?*
❏ *Did you use* **more** *or* **most** *with the adverbs that have two or more syllables?*

Lesson 32: **Using *Good* and *Well***

LEARN

The words *good* and *well* can sometimes be confusing.

Good is an adjective that describes a noun.
> Kim is a **good** cook.

Well is usually an adverb that describes a verb.
> She bakes **well**, too.

Well is an adjective only when it refers to someone's health. When *well* refers to health, it describes a noun.
> Kim was sick. She is **well** now.

Think about what you are describing when using *good* **and** *well.*

PRACTICE

A Underline the word in parentheses that correctly completes each sentence.

1. I'm afraid I don't cook very (good, well).

2. I thought I could make a (good, well) dinner from frozen leftovers.

3. I had promised my family a (good, well) meal.

4. Unfortunately, I didn't plan (good, well).

5. I should have taken a (good, well) look at the frozen foods.

6. I needed more time to cook them (good, well).

7. My cooking did not make a (good, well) impression on the family.

8. Fortunately, Dad had a (good, well) idea.

9. He knew that the microwave oven in the apartment next door worked (good, well).

10. We managed to cook the food quickly, thanks to our (good, well) neighbors.

B *Write **good** or **well** to complete each sentence.*

1. All young people should learn how to eat _____.

2. Cooking is a _____ skill to have.

3. Home-cooked, healthful meals help you stay _____.

4. Fast food from a restaurant isn't generally a _____ choice.

5. Cooking at home is a _____ way to save money.

6. Nutritious meals help a sick person get _____.

7. Making a _____ meal is relaxing.

8. There are many _____ ways to learn to cook.

9. Everyone knows at least one _____ cook.

10. Spend time with someone who cooks _____.

11. TV chefs prepare food very _____, too.

12. Reading cookbooks is another _____ idea.

13. In time, you will have many _____ recipes.

14. You will learn to serve meals _____.

15. There are plenty of _____ reasons to learn how to cook.

C Christopher wrote this restaurant recommendation for his aunt. He made six mistakes when using the words *good* and *well*. Use the proofreading marks in the box to correct the errors.

> If you're looking for a well restaurant, try the Lakeview House.
>
> First of all, the owners did a good job with decorating. Old signs and photographs cover the walls. Most nights, a jazz band plays. The bands play good, and the music goes good with the lakefront location. My mother wasn't feeling that well when we arrived, but the music soon cheered her up.
>
> There's always a good atmosphere at the Lakeview House. The waiters always treat the customers well. Most tables have a well view of the lake, too.
>
> Now for the most important thing—the food. My fish was delicious. It was cooked really good. Even the salad was good. Mom said her grilled chicken was good, too.
>
> The next time you want to eat out, try the Lakeview House. I think you'll have a well opinion of it, too.

Proofreading Marks

∧	Add
⊙	Period
℘	Take out
≡	Capital letter
/	Small letter

Did you correct six mistakes with *good* and *well*?

146 ■ Unit 4

WRITE

D *Imagine you are talking to a friend about food. Write two sentences you would say about each topic below. Use the word in parentheses in each sentence.*

1. your favorite fruit or vegetable

(good) _____

(well) _____

2. your favorite sandwich

(good) _____

(well) _____

3. your favorite home-cooked meal

(good) _____

(well) _____

4. your favorite dessert

(good) _____

(well) _____

Now imagine you are a nutritionist writing an article about healthy eating. How might the sentences you write for the article be different from the sentences above? Discuss this question with your classmates.

Proofreading Checklist ✔

❏ *Did you use the word **good** to describe nouns?*
❏ *Did you use the word **well** to describe verbs or to refer to someone's health?*

Lesson 33: **Negatives**

LEARN

■ A word that means "no" is called a **negative**. The words *no, not, nothing, none, never, nowhere, nobody,* and *no one* are negatives.

> Good manners **never** go out of style.
> There is **no** reason to behave rudely.

■ Contractions with *not*, such as *don't, wasn't,* and *aren't,* are also negatives.

> Many people **aren't** polite enough.
> They **don't** think about other people's feelings.

■ Do not use two negatives together in a sentence. This kind of mistake is called a **double negative**. To correct a sentence with a double negative, take out one negative or replace it with a word such as *any, every, ever, anything, anywhere, anyone,* or *anybody.*

> INCORRECT   **Don't never** talk during a movie.
>
> CORRECT   **Don't** talk during a movie.
> **Never** talk during a movie.
> **Don't ever** talk during a movie.

PRACTICE

A *Write the negative word in each sentence.*

1. Don't interrupt a speaker.   _____

2. Try not to call out answers in class.   _____

3. Booing another team doesn't show good sportsmanship.   _____

4. Nobody likes to lose a game.   _____

5. Still, there's nothing worse than a sore loser!   _____

6. There is no excuse for bad behavior.   _____

7. Never forget to say, "Please" and "Thank you."   _____

8. You shouldn't expect others to clean up after you.   _____

9. None of us should forget to write thank-you notes.   _____

10. There isn't any substitute for good manners.   _____

B *Write the word in parentheses that correctly completes each sentence.*

1. When it comes to manners, there isn't _____ as important as the dinner table. (anywhere, nowhere)

2. Don't go _____ too far when dinnertime is near. (anywhere, nowhere)

3. There isn't _____ in the kitchen. (no one, anyone)

4. No one _____ start eating before everyone is served. (should, shouldn't)

5. You should not _____ eat too fast. (ever, never)

6. There's never _____ excuse for gulping down food. (no, any)

7. Don't reach for _____ over someone else's plate. (nothing, anything)

8. Sometimes you don't like _____ on your plate. (nothing, anything)

9. Still, nobody wants to hear _____ rude comments about the food. (no, any)

10. You shouldn't _____ chew with your mouth open. (ever, never)

11. There shouldn't be _____ elbows on the table. (any, no)

12. There isn't _____ who can cook this well. (nobody, anybody)

C *Mariah wrote this essay about why manners are important. She used seven double negatives in her writing. Use the proofreading marks in the box to correct the errors.*

A lot of people today don't have no manners. They think that manners don't matter. That's where they're wrong.

Manners aren't just saying, "Please," or waiting your turn in line. Manners are about being kind and thoughtful. You don't want no one to interrupt you, so you shouldn't interrupt nobody else. It isn't no fun having someone cut in line in front of you, so you should never cut in front of nobody else.

People will judge you by your manners. If you don't have none, people will not think well of you. Even simple actions like saying, "Thank you," will make a good impression on others.

Good manners alone have never made no one a success. On the other hand, they haven't ever hurt anyone.

Proofreading Marks

∧	Add
⊙	Period
ℯ	Take out
≡	Capital letter
/	Small letter

Thank you!

Did you correct seven double negatives?

WRITE

D *Rewrite each sentence by adding a negative. Your sentences should give rules for good manners online. There may be more than one way to change each sentence. The first one is done for you.*

1. It's a good idea to type emails in all capital letters. *It's not a good idea to type emails in all capital letters. Or: Don't type emails in all capital letters.*

2. People who type in all capital letters are being thoughtful. _____

_____

3. Use busy-looking, colorful type and backgrounds in your emails. _____

_____

4. Busy-looking emails are easy to read. _____

_____

5. Leave the "Subject" line in an email blank. _____

_____

6. Some people want to receive email jokes and chain letters. _____

_____

7. Most of us want our mailboxes filled with junk mail. _____

_____

8. Open emails from people you don't know. _____

_____

Proofreading Checklist ✔

❏ *Did you add a negative to each sentence you wrote?*
❏ *Did you avoid double negatives in your sentences?*

Lesson 34: Prepositions and Prepositional Phrases

Snowshoe hare

LEARN

- A **preposition** is a word that shows how a noun or pronoun is connected to some other word in the sentence.

    The snowshoe hare lives **in** Alaska.
    During the summer, the hare's coat is brown.
    The hare's brown coat blends **with** the ground.

Here are some common prepositions.

about	among	below	for	near	through
above	around	beside	from	of	to
across	at	by	in	off	under
after	before	down	inside	on	until
against	behind	during	into	over	with

- A **prepositional phrase** is a group of words that begins with a preposition and ends with a noun or pronoun. When a prepositional phrase comes at the beginning of a sentence, it is followed by a comma.

    After the first snowfall, the hare's coat turns white.
    The hare **with the white coat** eats its meal.
    Another snowshoe hare sits **beside it**.

Prepositional phrases add important and interesting information to sentences.

PRACTICE

A Read each sentence. Look at each prepositional phrase in **boldface**. Write the preposition on the line.

1. I read a book **about camouflage**. _____

2. Camouflage lets an animal hide **from its predators**. _____

3. The chameleon lives **in Asia and Africa**. _____

4. Among green leaves, this lizard turns green.   _____

5. Above a brown branch, it turns brown.   _____

6. A giraffe has dark blotches **on its coat**.   _____

7. These blotches look like patches **of shade**.   _____

8. The giraffe is hard to see **under trees**.   _____

9. A fawn **with spots** is also hard to see.   _____

10. Light and shadows hide it **from view**.   _____

B *Underline the prepositional phrase in each sentence. Then write the preposition on the line.*

1. Some predators catch prey by surprise.   _____

2. Camouflage helps many of them.   _____

3. Frogs are hard to see on a green riverbank.   _____

4. They wait there for insects.   _____

5. The leaf-tailed gecko moves across the forest floor.   _____

6. To an insect, it could be a leaf.   _____

7. The arctic fox is white during the winter months.   _____

8. Quietly, it creeps over the snow.   _____

9. Fish below the water's surface can see the white feathers that cover a penguin's belly.   _____

10. These feathers look like the top of the water.   _____

11. This area gets bright light from the sun.   _____

12. Under the water, fish don't notice the penguin.   _____

C *Write a prepositional phrase to complete each sentence. Choose a prepositional phrase from the box, or use a prepositional phrase of your own. The first one is done for you.*

> in the dry grass   on the African plains   in snowy places
>
> down a river   against the snow   for a drink

1. Lion cubs live _____ *on the African plains*. _____

2. Their sandy-colored coats help them hide _____

3. Harp seal cubs live _____

4. Their snow-white coats can't be seen _____

5. A crocodile looks like a log floating _____

6. The crocodile doesn't move until some prey stops _____

> against the sand   in a swamp   with long necks
>
> in muddy water   of the desert   on its back

7. The turtle carries its home _____

8. _____, this shell looks like a rock.

9. Many desert birds are the color _____

10. Their enemies can't see them _____

11. Many swamp birds have thin bodies _____

12. These birds look like reeds _____

WRITE

D *One way to make a sentence more interesting and helpful to a reader is to add a prepositional phrase. Add a prepositional phrase to each sentence below.*

1. My friend loves desert animals. _____

_____

2. We visit the Natural History Museum. _____

_____

3. The museum has wonderful exhibits. _____

_____

4. We get a map when we arrive. _____

_____

5. Finally, we find the lizard exhibit. _____

_____

6. A plaque describes the snake fossils. _____

_____

7. A diagram gives more information. _____

_____

8. We spend more than an hour here. _____

_____

Go back to the prepositional phrases you added.
Circle the preposition in each one.

Adjectives (pp. 112–115) *Underline the adjective(s) in each sentence.*

1. Texas is a large state.

2. It has many famous landmarks.

3. The farmland is rich.

A, An, The; Demonstrative Adjectives (pp. 116–123) *Underline the word in parentheses that correctly completes each sentence.*

4. Dallas is (a, an) city in Texas.

5. We saw (a, an) astronaut in Houston.

6. (This, These) state produces many farm products.

7. (This, These) products include corn, wheat, and other grains.

8. The cotton is harvested by (that, those) workers.

Comparing with Adjectives (pp. 124–127) *Write the form of the adjective in parentheses that correctly completes each sentence.*

9. Only California has a (big) population than Texas.   _____

10. Gaudalupe Peak is the (high) mountain in Texas.   _____

11. Dallas is (large) than Austin.   _____

Comparing with *More* and *Most* (pp. 128–131) *Write **more** or **most** to complete each sentence.*

12. Of the many early Native Americans in Texas, the Caddos were

the _____ successful farmers.

13. The Jumano people are _____ famous for trading than for farming.

14. The Comanche were the _____ skillful hunters of all the groups.

Comparing with *Good* and *Bad* (pp. 132–135) *Write the form of the adjective in parentheses that correctly completes each sentence.*

15. The library has many (good) books about Texas. _____

16. This encyclopedia has (good) maps than that one. _____

17. This book is in the (bad) shape of all the books. _____

Adverbs (pp. 136–139) *Underline the adverb in each sentence.*

18. Spanish settlers reached Texas early.

19. They quickly built missions.

20. Texas was part of Mexico then.

Comparing with Adverbs (pp. 140–143) *Write the form of the adverb in parentheses that correctly completes each sentence.*

21. American settlers arrived in Texas (late) than Spanish settlers. _____

22. By 1830, Americans were settling Texas (quickly) than Mexicans were. _____

23. The American settlers could buy land (cheaply) in Texas than in the United States. _____

Using *Good* and *Well*; Negatives (pp. 144–151) *Underline the word in parentheses that correctly completes each sentence.*

24. Settlers came to Texas in search of a (good, well) life.

25. Farmers prepared their new fields (good, well).

26. Many Texans didn't want to be part of Mexico (no more, anymore).

27. No one could (ever, never) find a peaceful solution.

Prepositions and Prepositional Phrases (pp. 152–155) *Underline the prepositional phrase in each sentence. Then circle the preposition.*

28. For years, Texans opposed the Mexican government.

29. Later, Texas became part of the United States.

30. The history of Texas is long and interesting.

TIP 💡
Remember, you can find out more about adjectives, adverbs, and prepositions on pages 112–155.

PROOFREADING PRACTICE

Read the text below. There are 15 mistakes in the use of adjectives, adverbs, and prepositions. Use the proofreading marks in the box to correct them.

Proofreading Marks	
∧	Add
⊙	Period
ℒ	Take out
≡	Capital letter
/	Small letter

The woods around our town are filled birds and other animals. During the day, warblers sing prettily. At night, owls hoot. However, the town plans to build an road through the woods. I think this road plan would harm the woods and the wildlife terrible. It is not a well idea. We should replace it quick with a better plan.

The town says the road will affect only a smallest area. However, it will actual cut across the birds' main nesting area. Many plants that provide this birds with food will be removed.

In addition, construction will happen during the birds' nesting season. This season is the most busiest one for birds. It is the worse time to disturb them. People also hike in this here area. Adding a road will make it most dangerous for hikers.

In short, I think it would be gooder to build the road around the woods. This road would simple connect both sides of town. Then we do not never have to worry about causing harm.

WRITE ABOUT IT

Write an essay telling your opinion about building a road in the woods. Use details from the text on page 158. Include a variety of adjectives, adverbs, and prepositions in your text. Use the Writing Process Handbook on pages 236–251 to help you plan. When you are finished writing your draft, then proofread your work.

_____

_____

_____

_____

_____

_____

_____

Check It Out! ☑

Did you . . .
- ❏ *tell your opinion about building a road in the woods?*
- ❏ *use details from the text on page 158 in your essay?*
- ❏ *include a variety of adjectives, adverbs, and prepositions?*
- ❏ *avoid double negatives?*
- ❏ *revise and edit your writing to show what you learned about adjectives, adverbs, and prepositions?*
- ❏ *proofread for correct spelling, capitalization, and punctuation?*

TALK ABOUT IT

Discuss: *What have you seen on a visit to a wooded area? What did it sound and smell like? What did you do there? Use a variety of adjectives, adverbs, and prepositions to talk about your ideas.*

Lesson 35: **Subject Pronouns**

LEARN

- A **pronoun** is a word that takes the place of one or more nouns. A **subject pronoun** is used as the subject of a sentence. It tells *whom* or *what* the sentence is about.

  Jason visited Mount Rushmore.
  He photographed the giant sculpture.

  Mr. and Mrs. Gomez went with Jason.
  They enjoyed the trip.

Like nouns, subject pronouns can be singular or plural.

Singular	I	you	he	she	it
Plural	we	you	they		

Mount Rushmore

- A pronoun's **antecedent** is the noun the pronoun refers to. A pronoun and its antecedent must agree in number. If the antecedent is singular, the pronoun must be singular. If the antecendent is plural, the pronoun must be plural. In the first sentence below, the singular pronoun *she* refers to the singular noun *Elena*. In the second sentence, the plural pronoun *they* refers to *Mom and Dad*.

  Elena saw my photographs. **She** saw them yesterday.
  Mom and Dad enjoy traveling. **They** always travel by train.

PRACTICE

A   *Write the subject pronoun in each sentence.*

1. I visited Mount Rushmore with my grandmother.   _____

2. She lives in South Dakota.   _____

3. Have you ever been to Mount Rushmore?   _____

4. It shows the giant carved faces of four presidents.   _____

5. They are Washington, Jefferson, Lincoln, and Roosevelt.   _____

6. I also read about Gutzon Borglum.   _____

7. He designed the memorial.   _____

8. Did you know that workers carved with dynamite?   _____

9. They worked for fourteen years.   _____

10. We would like to go back someday.   _____

B *Write the subject pronoun that correctly completes each sentence.*

1. National memorials are places that honor important events.

_____ can be found all over our country.

2. The Wright Brothers National Memorial is in North Carolina.

_____ is a popular place to visit.

3. Orville Wright flew the first airplane.

_____ flew the plane for twelve seconds.

4. Sue visited the Lincoln Boyhood National Memorial in Indiana.

_____ learned that Abraham Lincoln's mother is buried there.

5. Visitors can see the log cabin and barn that sit on the grounds.

_____ can also see a living history demonstration that shows
what life was like then.

6. The Franklin Delano Roosevelt Memorial honors our 32nd president.

_____ has four outdoor rooms that trace the history of
FDR's four terms in office.

C *Here is an entry from Marsha's journal. Write a subject pronoun from the box to complete each sentence. You will use one pronoun more than once.*

I   you   he   she   it   we   they

Today, Uncle Jacob and I visited the Lewis and Clark National Historical Park. _____ thought the park
(1)
was really interesting.

Meriwether Lewis and William Clark were American explorers. _____ traveled across the United States
(2)
in 1804 and 1805. Their expedition included a young Native American woman named Sacagawea. _____ helped
(3)
guide the expedition.

In the afternoon, Uncle Jacob and _____ hiked a
(4)
two-mile trail through the park. There was something really special about this hike. _____ followed the same
(5)
path that Lewis and Clark took!

Uncle Jacob said historical sites teach you about history firsthand. _____ is right about that!
(6)

Did _____ know that the park is in two different
(7)
states? _____ are Washington and Oregon.
(8)

WRITE

Liberty Bell

Sometimes you might repeat the same nouns too many times in your sentences.

> Keiki went to Philadelphia. Keiki hoped to hear the Liberty Bell, but Keiki was disappointed. The Liberty Bell hasn't rung for more than 160 years.

You can use subject pronouns to replace some of the nouns. That way, your writing will sound smoother and less repetitive. Be sure each pronoun agrees with its antecedent.

> Keiki went to Philadelphia. **She** hoped to hear the Liberty Bell, but **she** was disappointed. **It** hasn't rung for more than 160 years.

D *Revise the sentences in these passages. Replace some of the nouns with subject pronouns. Watch for pronoun-antecedent agreement.*

1. Darla visited the Benjamin Franklin National Memorial in Philadelphia. Darla was amazed by the statue of Benjamin Franklin. The statue is 20 feet tall and weighs 30 tons. Franklin helped build our country. Franklin was a statesman and a writer. Franklin was also a scientist and inventor.

2. The Benjamin Franklin National Memorial holds many of Franklin's possessions. The Benjamin Franklin National Memorial also displays Franklin's early writings. Darla saw a Franklin stove there. Darla also saw the lightning rod that Franklin invented. The lightning rod saved many buildings from fire.

Lesson 36: **Pronoun-Verb Agreement**

LEARN

■ In every sentence, the verb must agree with the subject.

- When the subject pronoun is *he, she,* or *it,* add *-s* or *-es* to the present tense of most action verbs. If the verb ends in *y,* change the *y* to *i* before adding *-es.*
  He hurries to the campsite.
  She pitches the tent.
  It protects the campers from wind and rain.

- When the subject pronoun is *I, we, you,* or *they,* do not add *-s* or *-es* to the verb.
  I pack everything in my bag.
  We camp all the time.
  You start a campfire.
  They go for a swim.

PRACTICE

A *Write the verb in parentheses that correctly completes each sentence.*

1. I _____ across the lake with Mom. (paddle, paddles)

2. She _____ from the canoe. (fish, fishes)

3. We _____ two fish after a while. (catch, catches)

4. You _____ to Dan at the tent. (wave, waves)

5. He _____ to the dock. (rush, rushes)

6. I _____ back to camp. (race, races)

7. We _____ a campfire for Mom. (prepare, prepares)

8. She _____ the fish with Dan. (clean, cleans)

9. They _____ it over the fire. (fry, fries)

10. It _____ delicious! (taste, tastes)

B *Write the present tense of the verb in parentheses to correctly complete each sentence.*

1. We _____ our sleeping bags at sundown. (unroll)

2. You _____ mosquitoes in the tent. (hear)

3. They _____ loudly in Dan's ears. (buzz)

4. He _____ his arms and legs. (scratch)

5. I _____ all over, too. (itch)

6. He _____ the flashlight out to Mom. (bring)

7. She _____ the flashlight on. (switch)

8. It _____ for three seconds, and then it goes out. (shine)

9. We _____ lightning in the sky. (see)

10. It _____ brightly just before the raindrops start. (flash)

11. We _____ into our sleeping bags. (scurry)

12. They _____ slightly damp! (feel)

13. I _____ to get comfortable, but I'm lying on a rock. (try)

14. It _____ into my back all night. (push)

15. I _____ we have better luck tomorrow. (hope)

C *Charles wrote this essay about camping. He made seven mistakes in pronoun-verb agreement. Use the proofreading marks in the box to correct the errors.*

Remember 💡
A present-tense verb must agree with the subject pronoun.

Proofreading Marks

∧	Add
⊙	Period
ℓ	Take out
≡	Capital letter
/	Small letter

I like camping for many reasons. When you camp, you rely on your own skills to solve problems. Here are some examples. How do you find your way if you get lost in the woods? You uses a compass and a map. What do you do if your tent looks unsteady? You pitches it again and do a better job this time.

Camping also gives you a chance to relax. When my family camps, we leave our digital devices behind. I enjoys the silence, and so does my Mom. She try to write every day. I always carries a few books and spend time reading.

Camping is just plain fun, too. We sings songs and tell stories around the campfire. Mom watches for unusual birds. They flies around our camp sometimes. Other kinds of animals come close, too.

It's true that camping isn't always comfortable. Even so, it makes you feel great!

Did you correct seven verbs that did not agree with the pronouns?

Write
Your
Own

WRITE

D Look at the picture. Then write a sentence to tell what the person or thing named in parentheses is doing. Use a subject pronoun and a present-tense verb in each of your sentences. The first one is done for you.

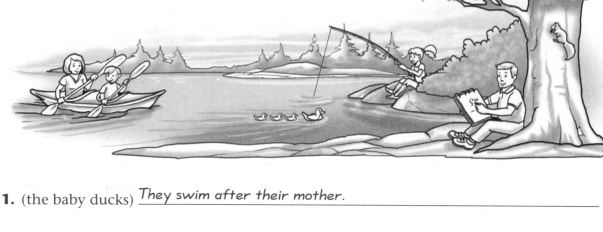

1. (the baby ducks) _They swim after their mother._ _____

_____

2. (the squirrel) _____

_____

3. (the girl) _____

_____

4. (the woman and the boy) _____

_____

5. (the man) _____

_____

Proofreading Checklist ✓

❑ Did you use subject pronouns for the subjects of your sentences?
❑ Did you use present-tense verbs?
❑ Did you check that your subjects and verbs agree?

Lesson 37: **Object Pronouns**

LEARN

- An **object pronoun** follows an action verb. It may also follow a word such as *to, in, at, of, with, during,* or *through*.

  I visited **the Washington Monument**.
  I visited **it**.

  Kim joined **my family and me** during our visit.
  Kim joined **us** during our visit.

  I had dinner with **my grandparents** afterward.
  I had dinner with **them** afterward.

- These are the object pronouns. Notice that the pronoun *you* can be singular or plural.

Singular	me	you	him	her	it
Plural	us	you	them		

Washington Monument

PRACTICE

A *Write the object pronoun in each sentence.*

1. My grandparents took me to Washington, D.C.   _____

2. A tour guide showed us the sights.   _____

3. "First, I will take you to the National Mall," the guide said.   _____

4. My grandmother asked her about the Washington Monument.   _____

5. Workers finished work on it in 1885.   _____

6. The bus had taken me past many tall buildings.   _____

7. The Washington Monument is the tallest of them all.   _____

8. A glass elevator whisked us to the top of the monument.   _____

9. "The guide will show you the Capitol next," Grandma said.   _____

10. "We will see it soon," I answered.   _____

B *Read each sentence. Replace the word or words in **boldface** with an object pronoun.*

1. Our nation's lawmakers meet in **the Capitol**.   _____

2. Some of **the lawmakers** were at work in the building.   _____

3. The Statue of Freedom stands on top of **the dome**.   _____

4. I followed **my grandfather** into the Rotunda.   _____

5. The huge round room impressed **my grandparents and me**.   _____

6. Thousands of people visit **the room** each day.   _____

7. I asked **my grandmother** about the large paintings in the Rotunda.   _____

8. One of **the paintings** shows the first reading of the Declaration of Independence.   _____

9. My grandmother pointed to **the statues of great Americans**.   _____

10. We looked closely at **one statue**.   _____

11. The person's face was familiar to **my grandmother and me**.   _____

12. Since 1986, the Rotunda has been home to this statue of **Dr. Martin Luther King, Jr**.   _____

C *Here is a description of a visit to the White House. Write an object pronoun from the box to complete each sentence. You will use some pronouns more than once.*

me	you	him	her	it	us	them

"More than a million people come to the White House every year," our guide told _____ at the start
(1)

of the tour. It seemed to _____ that most
(2)

of _____ were in our tour group!
(3)

I can only show _____ 5 of the 132 rooms
(4)

in the White House," the tour guide explained. "All of

_____ are on the first floor."
(5)

The most interesting room to _____
(6)

was the dining room. There are enough tables

and chairs in _____ for 140 dinner guests!
(7)

The president works downstairs in the West Wing, but

we didn't see _____. What about the first
(8)

lady? We didn't see _____ either.
(9)

The living area in the White House is upstairs,

but the tour guide couldn't take _____ there.
(10)

The only way I'll see that part of the White House is if

the country elects _____ president someday!
(11)

WRITE

Your writing will sound dull if you use the same nouns over and over again.

> The Lincoln Memorial honors Abraham Lincoln. It has a 19-foot statue of Abraham Lincoln inside.

When the overused nouns come after action verbs or after words such as *of* or *to*, you can replace them with object pronouns. Using object pronouns correctly will make your writing clearer and smoother.

> The Lincoln Memorial honors Abraham Lincoln. It has a 19-foot statue of **him** inside.

Lincoln Memorial

D *Revise the second sentence of each pair. Replace an overused noun in the second sentence with an object pronoun.*

1. Take a close look at a penny. The front of the penny shows Lincoln's face, and the back of the penny shows the Lincoln Memorial.

   _____

   _____

2. The Lincoln Memorial stands at the end of the National Mall. Many people think the Lincoln Memorial is the most beautiful monument in Washington, D.C.

   _____

   _____

3. Lincoln's famous words are carved on the monument. You can read Lincoln's famous words as you walk through the monument.

   _____

   _____

4. Lincoln looks sad to some visitors. Other visitors look at Lincoln and say he is smiling slightly.

   _____

   _____

Lesson 38: Using *I* and *Me*

LEARN

■ Be careful when you use the pronouns *I* and *me* in sentences. The pronoun *I* is a subject pronoun. *I* is used only as the subject of a sentence.

> **I** watch the stars with Adam and Rosa.

The pronoun *me* is an object pronoun. *Me* is used after an action verb or after a word such as *at, for, of, to,* or *with.*

> Rosa lends **me** a telescope.
> Adam names some stars for **me**.

■ When you speak about yourself and another person, always name the other person first. Then follow the rules above for when to use *I* and *me.*

> **Rosa and I** like astronomy.
> Brian shares a telescope with **Rosa and me**.
> At the park, **my friends and I** wait for the nighttime sky.

PRACTICE

A *Write the word or words in parentheses that correctly complete each sentence.*

1. Rosa invited _____ to a star-watching party. (Adam and I, Adam and me)

2. She showed _____ how to use a telescope. (I, me)

3. _____ found the Big Dipper. (I, Me)

4. Adam told _____ that there are 100 billion stars in our galaxy. (I, me)

5. _____ didn't even know that our sun is a star. (Rosa and I, Me and Rosa)

6. Adam showed _____ the star Sirius. (Brian and me, me and Brian)

7. _____ were amazed by its brightness! (Brian and I, Brian and me)

8. Brian asked _____ why the stars seem to twinkle. (I, me)

9. Adam explained the reason to _____. (the others and I, the others and me)

10. Now _____ are fascinated by the stars. (my friends and I, me and my friends)

B _Write **I** or **me** to correctly complete each sentence._

1. My twin sister Tina and _____ have a telescope.

2. Uncle George bought it for Tina and _____ last week.

3. Mom helped _____ assemble it.

4. My sister and _____ waited for a clear night.

5. Dad told _____ that starlight takes millions of years to reach Earth.

6. Tina and _____ found that hard to believe.

7. Mom pointed out the Great Bear constellation to Tina and _____.

8. That group of stars didn't look like a bear to _____.

9. My family and _____ visited the planetarium yesterday.

10. The guide showed my parents and _____ a model of the solar system.

11. She told _____ that the stars shine day and night.

12. Another guide gave _____ a book about the stars.

13. Both my sister and _____ learned many facts about outer space.

14. Learning about the stars has also inspired

_____.

15. _____ wrote a poem called "Starry Day" just yesterday.

The Great Bear (Ursa Major)

C Ray wrote this thank-you note to his uncle. He made seven mistakes when using the pronouns *I* and *me*. Use the proofreading marks in the box to correct the errors.

Dear Uncle George,

Tina and me want to thank you so much for the telescope! Mom helped I set it up last night. You couldn't have gotten me and Tina a better present! Fortunately, the nights are darker here than in most places. The whole family and me can get a great view of the night sky!

Please come visit my family and I soon! Tina and I will show you some stars and planets. Mom has already pointed out two planets, Venus and Mercury. With the telescope, I and Tina hope to spot Jupiter soon.

Thanks again,

Ray

P.S. Me and Tina also are using the sky chart that came with the telescope. It makes everything a lot easier!

Proofreading Marks

∧	Add
⊙	Period
ℒ	Take out
≡	Capital letter
/	Small letter

Did you correct seven mistakes with *I* and *me*?

WRITE

Pairs of related sentences can sound choppy when you read them. Try combining the sentences into one sentence that expresses the same idea. You can combine the sentences below by joining the noun in the subject of the first sentence and the subject pronoun in the second sentence.

> Tina invited Tim to our Planet Watch Party.
> I invited Tim to our Planet Watch Party.
> Tina **and** I invited Tim to our Planet Watch Party.

Sometimes you can combine related sentences by joining the noun that follows the action verb in the first sentence and the object pronoun in the second sentence.

> Tim thanked Tina.
> Tim thanked me.
> Tim thanked Tina **and** me.

D Combine each pair of sentences by joining a noun and a pronoun.

1. Dad showed Tim the planet Venus. I showed Tim the planet Venus.

_____

2. Kari lent her binoculars to Luke. Kari lent her binoculars to me.

_____

3. Venus looked so bright to Jessie. Venus looked so bright to me.

_____

4. Chris tried to find Jupiter. I tried to find Jupiter.

_____

5. The planets fascinate my friends. The planets fascinate me.

_____

Lesson 39: **Possessive Pronouns**

LEARN

- A possessive noun shows *who* or *what* has something. A **possessive pronoun** takes the place of a possessive noun.

  Heather's cat is a Siamese.
  Her cat is a Siamese.

- There are two kinds of possessive pronouns. One kind is used before a noun. The possessive pronouns that can be used before a noun are *my, your, his, her, its, our,* and *their.*

  My pet is a tabby cat.
  Your friend has three cats.
  Her cat won a ribbon.
  I love **their** beautiful coats.

  Its gray fur is so soft.
  The cat show was held in **our** town.

The other kind of possessive pronoun is used alone. The possessive pronouns that can stand alone are *mine, yours, his, hers, ours,* and *theirs.*

  The Persian cat is **hers**.
  The black kitten is **mine**.
  His is black, too.

  Theirs has white paws.
  This one is **ours**.
  Where is **yours**?

PRACTICE

A Underline the possessive pronoun in each sentence. Then write **before a noun** or **used alone** to tell how it is used.

1. The white cat is mine. _____

2. Siamese cats are known for their blue eyes. _____

3. Your cat is a calico. _____

4. Its coat has black, orange, and white patches. _____

5. Is this cat carrier yours? _____

6. Tonya says the Manx cat is hers. _____

7. Where is its tail? _____

8. Mr. Kubo brought his cat to the show.   _____

9. The large Burmese cat is his.   _____

10. Our cat show will be a great success.   _____

B *Write the possessive pronoun that correctly completes each sentence.*

1. _____ tabby cat has a yellow coat with dark stripes. (Her, Hers)

2. _____ cat weighs 23 pounds. (My, Mine)

3. Tails help cats keep _____ balance. (their, theirs)

4. One of the winning cats is _____. (her, hers)

5. _____ hair is short and curly. (It, Its)

6. The longhaired white cat is _____. (our, ours)

7. Which cat is _____? (your, yours)

8. _____ Maine Coon cat is larger than most. (Your, Yours)

9. The 20-year-old cat is _____. (my, mine)

10. The final decision is _____. (their, theirs)

11. I admire _____ independence and curiosity. (it, its)

12. Look at the painting of _____ cats. (our, ours)

C Sue wrote this report about a cat show she went to. She made seven mistakes using possessive pronouns. Use the proofreading marks in the box to correct the mistakes.

I have a tabby cat named Ali and a Persian cat named Timtam. Last week, I entered Timtam in a cat show. Timtam is a large male whose fur is long and shiny. Ali is a female, and hers fur has dark stripes. "Ours two cats are beautiful, but Timtam is the more unusual of the two," I told mine mother.

I carried Timtam to the show in a cat carrier. I had lined its sides with light blue silk to make Timtam look even better. At the show, my eyes widened, and mine mouth fell open. I had never seen so many cats!

"Is this cat your?" a judge asked me. "Yes, Timtam is mine," I replied. The judges studied Timtam carefully. Then they moved on to the other cats.

Timtam won a blue ribbon! I laughed and said to Timtam, "This is yours ribbon, but in a way, it's my, too. After all, we worked together to win it!"

Proofreading Marks

∧	Add
⊙	Period
℘	Take out
≡	Capital letter
/	Small letter

Did you correct seven possessive pronouns?

WRITE

D *Read each short description, and imagine the scene. Then write
two sentences to tell more about what is happening. Use a
possessive pronoun in each sentence. The first one is done for you.*

1. Two cats are asleep on a sofa.

The cats sleep in their favorite place.

Each cat enjoys its nap.

2. A girl is brushing the long hair of a cat.

_____

_____

3. Two judges are awarding a ribbon to a prize-winning cat.
The cat's owners are standing nearby.

_____

_____

4. A boy pulls a piece of string to play with a pet cat.

_____

_____

5. A mother cat washes the small kittens.

_____

_____

6. A cat watches while a woman opens a can.

_____

_____

Proofreading Checklist

❏ *Did you use the correct possessive pronoun in
each sentence?*

Lesson 40: Relative Pronouns and Relative Adverbs

LEARN

■ In a complex sentence, the second idea is related to the first idea. Sometimes the second idea is introduced by a relative pronoun. The **relative pronoun** relates the two ideas, linking the second idea to a noun in the first idea.

- Abbey is the girl **who** is on our swim team.

- She is the person **that** brought the team to victory.

- The swim cap **which** (or **that**) she lost has red and white stripes.

- This is the team **whose** coach was honored.

- He is the coach **whom** we met last year.

When talking about people, use *who, whom,* or *that.* When talking about things, use *that* or *which.* To show who something belongs or relates to, use *whose.*

■ Sometimes the **relative adverbs** *where, when,* and *why* introduce the second idea. Use **where** after the word *place* or place words such as *room* or *street.* Use **when** after the word *time* or time words such as *day* or *year.* Use **why** after *reason.*

- This is the pool **where** the team practices.

- There was a time **when** we practiced outdoors.

- There is no reason **why** we can't try again.

PRACTICE

A *Underline the relative pronoun or relative adverb in each sentence.*

1. The swim meet which takes place at our school is always the most thrilling!

2. The swimming events are the only ones that take place indoors.

3. I found the lane where my relay partner was warming up.

4. Angela is the girl with whom I swim in the relay race.

5. There is a good reason why the other team arrived so late.

6. The first race starts at 1 p.m. when everyone is on her mark.

7. The judge who explains the rules was one of the coaches last year.

8. The team that gets the most points will go to the state championships.

9. The team whose mascot is a dolphin won the most medals.

10. We will get our medals tomorrow when we have our team dinner.

B *Write the relative pronoun or relative adverb in parentheses that correctly completes each sentence.*

1. Olympic athletes are the people _____ I look up to the most. (which, whom)

2. Kim is the girl _____ parents were both Olympic swimmers. (who, whose)

3. She trains at the sports arena _____ has an Olympic size swimming pool. (which, who)

4. Roberto is the young man _____ beat the state record for the 50-meter butterfly. (which, who)

5. The butterfly is a stroke _____ may seem difficult at first. (that, whom)

6. The lake near my house is _____ Roberto learned to swim. (when, where)

7. Roberto joined the Men's U.S. Olympic team the year _____ it won six gold medals. (when, why)

8. His dream of becoming an Olympic champion is the reason

_____ he practices so much. (where, why)

C *Here is a description of a baseball game played at a sports festival. Write a relative pronoun or relative adverb from the box to complete each sentence.*

who	when	whose	why
that	where	which	whom

For the first game of the season, the Jonestown Lions played the Smithfield Tigers. The Tigers were the team _____ won the district championship last year. Its players are the best in the league.

The game started and the Lions were the first to bat. Lucas is the team's star batter _____ arms are so strong he can knock the ball out of the park. On the first pitch, he hit the ball long and hard. As he slid into home, the umpire called, "Out!"

Lucas asked him for the reason _____ he had made that call. The umpire said the left fielder had caught the ball the moment _____ Lucas began his slide into home. Lucas could not believe it.

In disbelief, Lucas went back to the dugout _____ his team was sitting. It was a call _____ no one would forget. It was still a close game _____ ended with the Lions' first win over the Tigers!

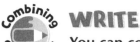
Combining Sentences

WRITE

You can combine two related sentences with a relative pronoun or relative adverb. When you combine sentences in this way, you avoid repeating words.

> The Red Rockets is a soccer team. The soccer team participated in the South Shore tournament.
> The Red Rockets is the soccer team **that** participated in the South Shore tournament.
>
> My dad drove me to the soccer field. My team was getting ready for the game there.
> My dad drove me to the soccer field **where** my team was getting ready for the game.

D *Read each pair of sentences. Use the relative pronoun or relative adverb in parentheses to combine the sentences. Write the new sentence on the line.*

1. We spotted the player. We admire her the most. (whom) _____

_____

2. Rachel is the new player. She joined our team last weekend. (who) _____

_____

3. Mr. Arnold is the coach. His job is to improve our soccer skills. (whose) _____

_____

4. Dribbling is a skill. It requires a lot of practice. (that) _____

_____

5. No one knows the reason. The referee cancelled the game. (why) _____

_____

6. Frosty's is the ice cream shop. My team goes there after every

game. (where) _____

_____

Lesson 41: **Contractions with Pronouns**

LEARN

■ A **contraction** is made by joining two words together. An apostrophe (') takes the place of any letters that are left out.

Many contractions are formed by joining a pronoun and a verb.

Pronoun and Verb	Contraction	Pronoun and Verb	Contraction
I am	**I'm**	I have	**I've**
she is	**she's**	she has	**she's**
it is	**it's**	it has	**it's**
you are	**you're**	you have	**you've**
they are	**they're**	they have	**they've**
I will	**I'll**	I had	**I'd**
you will	**you'll**	you had	**you'd**
we will	**we'll**	we had	**we'd**
they will	**they'll**	they had	**they'd**

■ Be especially careful when you use the contractions *he's,* *she's,* and *it's.* The contractions for *he, she,* and *it* and the verbs *is* and *has* are the same.

It is time to go home.	I think **he is** the best writer.
It's time to go home.	I think **he's** the best writer.
It has been a busy day.	We know that **he has** won the prize.
It's been a busy day.	We know that **he's** won the prize.

PRACTICE

A *Write the contraction for each pair of words.*

1. I am _____

2. you will _____

3. he is _____

4. we are _____

5. they had _____

6. I have _____

7. they are _____

9. we had _____

8. she has _____

10. it has _____

B *Read each sentence. Replace the pronoun and verb in **boldface** with a contraction.*

1. I am Becky's friend. _____

2. You are Becky's friend, too. _____

3. She is at the National Spelling Bee in Washington, D.C. _____

4. We will meet her at the airport when she returns. _____

5. She has never been to Washington, D.C. _____

6. You have visited many times. _____

7. You will have plenty to talk about. _____

8. It is the day of Becky's flight. _____

9. We had better hurry, or we will be late. _____

10. I wish **I had** checked the schedule earlier. _____

11. I hope **she will** arrive late. _____

12. It has taken us an hour to get to the airport. _____

13. They are Becky's mom and dad. _____

14. I think **he is** Becky's brother. _____

15. I see that **we are** not late after all. _____

C A group of students collected these sayings and bits of advice from their friends and family members. While listing the sayings, they made eight mistakes when using contractions. Use the proofreading marks in the box to correct the errors.

- It's called common sense, but its always very rare.

- If you don't believe in something, youll' fall

  for anything.

- Hed tried to have it both ways and ended up

  with neither.

- Fish don't get caught if theyve kept their mouths shut.

- We'll have to break some eggs to make an omelet.

- Id rather wear out than rust.

- If you nurse your troubles, theyll only grow larger.

- It's better to give than to receive.

- Your'e going to catch more flies with honey than

  with vinegar.

- Teach people to fish, and theyr'e fed for a lifetime.

Proofreading Marks

∧	Add
⊙	Period
⤶	Take out
≡	Capital letter
/	Small letter

Did you correct eight contractions?

Write Your Own

WRITE

D *Imagine that you are writing an ad for a new laundry detergent called Supersuds. Write some sentences that might appear in your ad. In each sentence, include the contraction in parentheses. The first one is done for you.*

1. (it's) *It's the best laundry detergent ever!*
_____

2. (she's) _____
_____

3. (we've) _____
_____

4. (I've) _____
_____

5. (they've) _____
_____

6. (you'll) _____
_____

7. (I'm) _____
_____

8. (you're) _____
_____

Now imagine that you are a scientist writing a review of Supersuds for a newspaper. How might the sentences you write for the review be different from the sentences above? Discuss this question with your classmates.

Proofreading Checklist ✓

❏ *Did you use a contraction in each sentence you wrote?*
❏ *Did you spell each contraction correctly?*

Subject Pronouns (pp. 160–163) *Write the subject pronoun in each sentence.*

1. I have two friends who are unable to hear. _____

2. They communicate with American Sign Language. _____

3. It is also known as ASL. _____

4. We speak this language together. _____

Pronoun-Verb Agreement (pp. 164–167) *Underline the verb in parentheses that correctly completes each sentence.*

5. I (practice, practices) the ASL finger alphabet with Terry.

6. We (spell, spells) our names.

7. She (teach, teaches) me with the help of a chart.

8. It (show, shows) all the letters.

Object Pronouns (pp. 168–171) *Write the object pronoun in each sentence.*

9. Sign language helps us in many ways. _____

10. It helps my friends talk to me. _____

11. I can tell them jokes using ASL. _____

12. We wouldn't communicate as well without it. _____

Using *I* and *Me* (pp. 172–175) *Underline the word or words in parentheses that correctly complete each sentence.*

13. Jim and (I, me) know some Braille.

14. Grandma taught my cousin and (I, me) about this writing system.

15. Grandma showed her Braille writer to (me and Jim, Jim and me).

16. (Jim and I, Jim and me) like to use this machine sometimes.

Possessive Pronouns (pp. 176–179) *Write the possessive pronoun in each sentence.*

17. Louis Braille invented his famous alphabet in 1829. _____

18. Blind readers use their fingers to read raised dots on paper. _____

19. Each group of dots has its own meaning. _____

20. Is this Braille book yours? _____

Relative Pronouns and Relative Adverbs (pp. 180–183)
Write the relative pronoun or relative adverb in parentheses that correctly completes each sentence.

21. Mr. Niles is the school custodian _____ job it is to post all Braille signs. (who, whose)

22. The new elevator at the school is the place _____ a Braille sign was just posted. (when, where)

23. Our teacher purchased a Braille labeler last year _____ the class started to learn about Braille. (when, why)

24. Helen Keller is a well-known person _____ raised money for the blind. (whom, who)

Contractions with Pronouns (pp. 184–187) *Read each sentence. Write a contraction for the pronoun and verb in **boldface**.*

25. **They have** put the chart of Braille letters on the wall. _____

26. **He is** touching the dots with his finger. _____

27. I think **it is** the letter *a*. _____

28. **She has** found the dots for the word *hello*. _____

TIP 💡

Remember, you can find out more about
pronouns and contractions on pages 160–187.

PROOFREADING PRACTICE

*Read the text below. There are 15 mistakes in the use of pronouns and
contractions. Use the proofreading marks in the box to correct them.*

Proofreading Marks

∧	Add
⊙	Period
ℐ	Take out
≡	Capital letter
/	Small letter

I gazed in amazement at my school library. Its was

filled with art for the school art show. I set up me

artwork and then wandered off to check out the show.

First, I went to see the sculptures. My friend Ted

was surrounded by clay dragons! I thought he'd made

they all. Ted pointed out which ones were him. Ted's dragons had

eyes that sparkled. They're teeth glowed.

Next, I visited the paintings. There was a huge painting of a

shark. I wondered who's it was. Then I saw a boy wearing a shirt

with a fish on her. He and me talked about sharks for a while.

Finally, I went back to my artwork, which was a picture

frame that they'd made myself. People crowded around. Them

wondered why the frame was empty. So I asked whom would

like to be the picture! A girl held my frame in his hands and

looked through it. I took her picture with mine camera. "Who'll go

next?" I asked. "Us will!" replied the crowd. By the end of the

show, I'll taken lots of pictures of people with my picture frame!

WRITE ABOUT IT

Write a story about someone else whose art is in the same school art show. Use details from the text on page 190. Include a variety of pronouns in your story. Use the Writing Process Handbook on pages 236–251 to help you plan. When you are finished writing your draft, then proofread your work.

_____

_____

_____

_____

_____

_____

_____

Check It Out! ☑

Did you . . .

❑ write about someone else who has artwork in the show?

❑ use details from the text on page 190 in your story?

❑ include a beginning, middle, and end to your story?

❑ revise and edit your writing to show what you learned about pronouns?

❑ proofread for correct spelling, capitalization, and punctuation?

TALK ABOUT IT

Discuss: What kind of art do you like to make? What kind of artwork do you like to see? What art would you share in a school art show? Explain. Use a variety of pronouns to talk about your ideas.

Lesson 42: **Writing Sentences Correctly**

LEARN

■ When you write, you must show where each sentence begins and ends.

Begin every sentence with a capital letter, and end every sentence with a punctuation mark. The end punctuation you use depends on the kind of sentence you write.

Scientist installing part of an earthquake warning system

- End a declarative sentence with a **period (.)**.
  About a million earthquakes occur each year.

- End an interrogative sentence with a **question mark (?)**.
  Are there really that many?

- End an exclamatory sentence with an **exclamation mark (!)**.
  What a huge number that is!

- End an imperative sentence with a **period (.)**.
  Read this article about earthquakes.

■ When you rewrite a run-on sentence as two separate sentences, be sure to use capital letters and end punctuation marks correctly.

RUN-ON	Can earthquakes be predicted scientists are working on a warning system.
CORRECTED SENTENCE	Can earthquakes be predicted? Scientists are working on a warning system.

PRACTICE

A *Read each item. Write **correct** or **incorrect** to tell whether the sentence or sentences are written correctly.*

1. Most earthquakes occur under the sea. How lucky that is! _____

2. Why do you say that _____

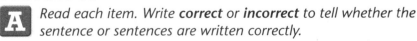

3. most underwater earthquakes are never even noticed _____

4. Large underwater earthquakes can cause tsunamis
The results can be very dangerous _____

5. What is a *tsunami*? It's a Japanese word for a huge wave. _____

6. all earthquakes occur along fault lines in the earth's crust _____

7. Have you ever felt an earthquake usually the ground
shakes gently. _____

8. Large earthquakes make loud, rumbling noises. _____

9. most earthquakes last less than a minute _____

10. Smaller aftershocks can rattle for days afterward. _____

B *Write these sentences correctly. Use capital letters and the correct end punctuation marks. Write each run-on sentence as two sentences.*

1. scientists use the Richter scale to measure the strength of earthquakes _____

_____

2. look at this chart of measurements the scale goes from 0 to 10 _____

_____

3. earthquakes below 5 usually don't cause much damage _____

_____

4. do you see the 9.5 on the chart _____

_____

5. that is the measurement for the biggest earthquake ever the earthquake occurred in

Chile in 1960 _____

_____

Remember 💡
Begin every sentence with a capital letter. Use the correct end punctuation for each of the four kinds of sentences.

On April 18, 1906, the sun had just risen most people in San Francisco were asleep. Some were getting ready for work.

Suddenly a loud roar filled the air. The ground was shaking, and buildings and power lines were falling. What was happening A huge earthquake was tearing the city apart.

Gas poured out of broken gas lines. Fires broke out everywhere How disastrous they would be Why weren't the fires put out The water lines had broken, too.

After three days, the fires were finally out the shaking had stopped, too. Over 25,000 buildings had fallen. about 490 city blocks had been destroyed.

What lessons did people learn from this disaster? They learned to build stronger buildings they decided to use more flexible pipes, too. What a difference these changes would make in the future

Proofreading Marks

∧	Add
⊙	Period
ℒ	Take out
≡	Capital letter
/	Small letter

San Francisco, 1906

Did you correct four mistakes in capitalization and eight mistakes in end punctuation?

WRITE

D *Read each explanation below about earthquake safety.
Then write a statement, command, exclamation,
or question you might say to respond to each explanation.
The word in parentheses tells you what kind of sentence
to write. The first one is done for you.*

1. Earthquakes can be dangerous. Fortunately, there are some
important steps you can take to reduce the danger. (question)

What steps can I take to reduce the danger?

_____

2. Identify the "danger zones" in your house. These include areas
with windows, tall furniture, and heavy objects. These things are
dangerous during an earthquake. (exclamation)

_____

_____

3. You should be aware of safe spots, such as a sturdy desk or table,
in a room. They provide cover from falling objects. (question)

_____

_____

4. If you are outside, move away from tall buildings and power lines.
If possible, go to an open space or park. (command)

_____

_____

5. Most people will never experience a serious earthquake.
Still, it's a good idea to be prepared. (statement)

_____

_____

Lesson 43: Capitalizing Proper Nouns

LEARN

A **proper noun** names a specific person, place, or thing. Each important word in a proper noun begins with a capital letter.

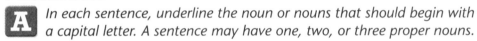

- The names of people, pets, and special groups always begin with a capital letter.
  Darren Smith   Sparky   Little League

- The names of special places begin with a capital letter.
  Elm Street   Overton Park   Canada
  Detroit   New Mexico   Mills Elementary School

- The names of days, months, and holidays begin with a capital letter.
  Tuesday   November   Election Day

- Family titles that refer to specific people begin with a capital letter.
  Grandma   Uncle Dave   Aunt Sue

- Titles of respect that are used with names begin with a capital letter.
  Mr. Luna   Ms. Elkins   Mayor Quinn   President Roosevelt

PRACTICE

A *In each sentence, underline the noun or nouns that should begin with a capital letter. A sentence may have one, two, or three proper nouns.*

1. The last monday in may is memorial day.

2. People from maine to california honor those who gave their lives for our country.

3. The holiday began in 1866 in waterloo, new york.

4. At that time, it was called decoration day.

5. Different states celebrated this holiday in april, may, and june.

6. In 1971, memorial day became a legal holiday throughout the united states.

7. This year, dennis and I marched with the cub scouts in a parade.

8. The parade began at lakehurst elementary school.

9. It ended on main street.

10. Ms. hernandez led the band, and mayor dixon gave a speech.

B *Rewrite each sentence. Capitalize each proper noun correctly.*

1. The fourteenth day of june is called flag day. _____

_____

2. On that day in 1777, our country's leaders met in philadelphia and adopted the first flag. _____

_____

3. In 1885, a teacher named bernard cigrand suggested a holiday called flag birthday. _____

_____

4. President harry truman made flag day an official holiday in 1949. _____

_____

5. We celebrate a different national holiday in july. _____

_____

6. The holiday is called independence day. _____

_____

7. Our country declared its freedom from great britain on july 4, 1776. _____

_____

C *Mitchell wrote this report about Labor Day. He forgot to capitalize seven proper nouns, and he capitalized one common noun by mistake. Use the proofreading marks in the box to correct the errors.*

Many holidays honor famous leaders such as abraham Lincoln and Martin Luther King, Jr. The first monday in September, however, honors ordinary working people.

How did this Holiday begin? Two hard-working men get the credit. One was a carpenter in New York. The other was a machine operator in Paterson, new Jersey. Both men wanted everyone to appreciate how hard some people work. In september 1882, they organized a big parade for workers in New York city.

The idea of honoring workers caught on. In 1887, Oregon was the first state to make Labor Day a holiday. In 1894, president Grover Cleveland made it a national holiday. Other countries have similar holidays. In Australia, people celebrate Eight Hour Day. It honors the successful struggle for a shorter working day. In most of the world, a workers' holiday is celebrated on the first day in may.

Proofreading Marks

∧	Add
⊙	Period
ℓ	Take out
≡	Capital letter
/	Small letter

Did you correct eight mistakes in capitalization?

WRITE

D *Think about the holidays listed below. Write a few sentences to explain why we celebrate each holiday. Tell how you might celebrate the holiday at school or at home. Use proper nouns in your sentences.*

1. Martin Luther King, Jr., Day _____

_____

_____

_____

2. Presidents' Day _____

_____

_____

_____

3. Thanksgiving _____

_____

_____

_____

4. New Year's Eve _____

_____

_____

_____

Proofreading Checklist

❑ *Did you use proper nouns in your sentences?*
❑ *Did you begin each important word in a proper noun with a capital letter?*

Lesson 44: **Abbreviations**

LEARN

- An **abbreviation** is a short way of writing a word. Many abbreviations begin with a capital letter and end with a period. Here are some of them.

Titles of Respect

Ms. Margaret Wong   **Mr.** Alberto Mador   **Dr.** Susan Lewis

Addresses

St. (Street)   **Ave.** (Avenue)   **Rd.** (Road)
Blvd. (Boulevard) **Rte.** (Route)   **P.O.** (Post Office)

Months and Days of the Week

May, June, and *July* do not have abbreviations.

Jan. Feb. Mar. Apr. Aug. Sept. Oct. Nov. Dec.
Sun. Mon. Tues. Wed. Thurs. Fri. Sat.

- An **initial** is used in place of a name. It is written as a capital letter followed by a period.

Kim Ann Chin   **John Edward** Murphy
Kim A. Chin   **J. E.** Murphy

- State names that are used with ZIP codes have special two-letter abbreviations. Both letters are capitalized, and no period is used.

AL (Alabama)   **CA** (California)

PRACTICE

A *Write each name or abbreviation correctly.*

1. Jan 11 _____

2. dr ellen rossi _____

3. 201 Milton ave. _____

4. Feb 21, 2013 _____

5. rte. 202 _____

6. Elm st _____

7. mon _____

8. mr L M Kent _____

9. Oakland, ca _____

10. PO. Box 112 _____

B *Read each item below. Follow the directions in parentheses to change it. Use capital letters and periods correctly.*

1. Joan Richards _____
(Change the first name to an initial.)

2. 863 Clayton Avenue _____
(Use an abbreviation.)

3. 27 Red Rock Boulevard _____
(Use an abbreviation.)

4. Saturday, March 5 _____
(Use two abbreviations.)

5. Ms. June Marie Garcia _____
(Change the first and middle names to initials.)

6. Mobile, Alabama 36601 _____
(Use an abbreviation.)

7. Post Office Box 1413 _____
(Use an abbreviation.)

8. Closed: Saturday,
Sunday, and Monday _____
(Use three abbreviations.)

9. 192 Village Road _____
(Use an abbreviation.)

10. Doctor Makara Bel Singh _____
(Use an abbreviation and two initials.)

C Look at the items below. In each one, some of the abbreviations are written incorrectly. In two of the items, the initials are also written incorrectly. Altogether, there are eleven errors. Use the proofreading marks in the box to correct the errors.

Remember
Most abbreviations begin with a capital letter and end with a period.

Proofreading Marks

∧	Add
⊙	Period
ℒ	Take out
≡	Capital letter
/	Small letter

1.

Mr Arthur m. Nagel

41 Hillside ave.

Los Angeles, Ca 90102

2. Bennett rd.

3. Jackson Ave

4.

Welcome to the Ellen S King Library

Library Hours: Mon — Thurs.   9–5

fri. — Sat.   9–4

Closed Sun.

5.

Date _____ Apr 14 _____

For _____ Sally _____

_____ Josh _____ called.

Message _____ Don't forget to bring your _____

_____ rock collection to school on tues. _____

Did you correct a total of eleven mistakes?

WRITE

D Imagine that a cousin named Jackie is visiting you. You took each telephone message described below for her. Fill in the message pad with the missing information. Use abbreviations whenever possible. Part of the first one is done for you.

1. Doctor Clement's office called on August 24 to ask if Jackie can change her dental appointment from August 31 to September 1 at 10 o'clock.

> Date _____ *Aug. 24* _____
>
> For _____ *Jackie* _____
>
> _____ called.
>
> Message _____
>
> _____
>
> _____

2. Jackie's friend Anna called on August 25. She wants to know if Jackie can come to a book club meeting this Thursday at 4:30 at the Gomez's house at 240 Kent Road.

> Date _____
>
> For _____
>
> _____ called.
>
> Message _____
>
> _____
>
> _____

Lesson 45: **Titles**

LEARN

- Titles of books, magazines, and newspapers are set off by italics in printed material. When you write by hand, underline these titles.

PRINTED	*Middletown News* **(newspaper)**
HANDWRITTEN	<u>Middletown News</u>

PRINTED	*James and the Giant Peach* **(book)**
HANDWRITTEN	<u>James and the Giant Peach</u>

- Titles of songs and most poems are set off by quotation marks.

    "Home on the Range" **(song)**   "The Farmer in the Dell" **(song)**
    "Casey at the Bat" **(poem)**   "What Is Pink?" **(poem)**

- Notice that the first word and each important word in the titles begin with a capital letter. Words such as *a, an, at, and, by, for, in, of, on, the, to,* and *with* are not capitalized unless they are the first or last word in the title.

PRACTICE

A *Write each title correctly.*

1. elmsford journal (newspaper) _____

2. highlights for children (magazine) _____

3. the sound of music (song) _____

4. my side of the mountain (book) _____

5. paul revere's ride (poem) _____

6. a bicycle built for two (song) _____

7. who has seen the wind? (poem) _____

8. national geographic for kids (magazine) _____

9. the adventures of Tom Sawyer (book) _____

10. hudson valley news (newspaper) _____

B *Write the title in each sentence on the line. Capitalize each title. Also underline or add quotation marks to set off the title.*

1. I just read this month's sports illustrated for kids. _____

_____

2. oodles of noodles is a funny poem. _____

_____

3. We sang I've been working on the railroad in music class. _____

_____

4. A mouse acts bravely in the book mrs. frisby and the rats of NIMH. _____

_____

5. If you like funny books about school, read amber brown is not a crayon. _____

_____

6. your big backyard is a magazine for very young readers. _____

_____

7. There was an old man with a beard is a short and funny poem. _____

_____

8. The magazine stone soup publishes stories by children. _____

_____

9. The fans sang happy days are here again at the end of the game. _____

_____

C Alexander wrote this review of the school talent show. He made seven mistakes when writing titles. Use the proofreading marks in the box to correct the errors.

Did you ever wonder if the students in our school are talented? Last night's talent show proved that we are.

Dylan got the show off to a great start! He played "on the Sunny Side of the Street" on the trumpet. Terry played "Sandpipers on the beach" on the flute. The sad, beautiful sound of her instrument filled the auditorium. Finally, Roxanne's fiddle version of "Turkey In the Straw" had us tapping our feet.

A few students read aloud. Jacob had memorized the poem Stopping by Woods on a Snowy Evening" by Robert Frost. Maya read a funny passage from her favorite book, Alice's Adventures in Wonderland.

The singers were great, too. Patrick sang "Give My Regards To Broadway." Gina also did a great job. She sang "my Favorite Things" while playing a guitar.

All in all, it was a great show. I don't think anyone can say that our students lack talent.

Proofreading Marks

∧	Add
⊙	Period
ℒ	Take out
≡	Capital letter
/	Small letter

Did you correct seven mistakes in the titles?

WRITE

D *Read each description of a make-believe book, song, or poem. Then make up a title for it. Write your title on the line. The first one is done for you.*

1. a poem about a boy who likes to climb trees with his cat _____

"Up in the Branches"

2. a song about paddling a canoe on a river _____

_____

3. a magazine for children who like to collect stamps and coins _____

_____

4. a book about two identical twins who play tricks on their classmates _____

_____

5. a poem about the start of a new school year _____

_____

6. a magazine for people who want to help and protect endangered animals _____

_____

7. a song about a big family get-together in the summer _____

_____

8. a book about an immigrant family coming to the United States in 1900 _____

_____

9. a poem about a snowstorm that drops two feet of snow on your neighborhood

_____

Proofreading Checklist ☑

❑ *Did you begin the first word in each title with a capital letter?*
❑ *Did you begin each important word in a title with a capital letter?*

Lesson 46: **Commas in a Series**

LEARN

A **comma** separates words or ideas in a sentence and tells the reader when to pause.

Sometimes a sentence has a **series**, or list, of three or more items. Use a comma to separate the items in a series.

> Our **teachers, parents, and classmates** planned a field day.

> The event took place on a **beautiful, warm, sunny** Saturday.

> I brought **sunglasses, a hat, and some sunscreen**.

> To get to the park, many people **walked, biked, or drove**.

Do not use a comma after the last word in the series.

PRACTICE

A   *In each sentence, the items in a series are in **boldface**. Add commas to separate the items.*

1. Parents organized **races contests and activities**.

2. People played **softball volleyball and basketball**.

3. I **pitched batted and scored** in the softball game.

4. **Friends relatives and pets** sat nearby and watched us play.

5. **Jess Mario and Kate** hit home runs.

6. For lunch, my Dad grilled the **hamburgers hot dogs and ribs**.

7. I put **lettuce tomato and ketchup** on my hamburger.

8. The ribs tasted **hot spicy and delicious**.

9. Everyone **gnawed nibbled munched and crunched** corn on the cob.

10. For dessert, we ate **big ripe juicy** peaches.

B *Underline the items in a series in each sentence. Then add commas to separate the items.*

1. At the field day, the fishing contest was for parents teachers and students.

2. Blue red and yellow ribbons had been prepared for the winners.

3. I had brought my rod tackle and bait.

4. I hummed whistled and waited for a bite.

5. I caught a small wet wiggly trout right away.

6. It had a blue green and silver back.

7. Next, I hooked two sunfish a catfish and a crab.

8. I threw them back, and they flopped splashed and swam toward the rock.

9. My rod suddenly twitched jerked and pulled.

10. I had hooked a big strong lively bass!

11. I tugged strained and reeled it in.

12. Parents students and the judge gathered around.

13. No one else had caught such a big healthy beautiful bass.

14. I didn't want to carry clean and cook it.

15. Everyone cheered clapped and shouted when I let it go.

C *Paula saw this list of rules at the park. The list contains twelve mistakes in the use of commas in a series. Some commas were left out, and some appear where they don't belong. Use the proofreading marks in the box to correct the errors.*

Proofreading Marks

∧	Add
⊙	Period
ℒ	Take out
≡	Capital letter
/	Small letter

PARK RULES

✪ The trees shrubs and wildflowers in this park are protected. Visitors should not cut, damage or remove any plant.

✪ The hunting trapping or harming of animals is forbidden. Fishing in the pond and streams is permitted.

✪ Walking jogging, and bicycling are permitted, on park trails.

✪ Horseback riding is permitted on marked trails. Visitors should not lead, ride or walk a horse in other areas of the park.

✪ No one is permitted to sell, food, drinks, or other items in the park.

✪ Park fireplaces stoves and grills may be used in picnic areas. No one is permitted to light build, or maintain a fire in other areas of the park.

Did you correct twelve mistakes in the use of commas in a series?

WRITE

Sometimes you can use a series to combine short, choppy
sentences to make your writing smoother. The underlined words
in each sentence below tell what games the children played.
You can put the words in a series to make one smooth sentence.

> The young children played <u>tag</u>.
> They played <u>hopscotch</u>.
> They played <u>dodgeball</u>.
>
> The young children played <u>tag</u>, <u>hopscotch</u>, **and** <u>dodgeball</u>.

You can also put groups of words in a series.

> The parents <u>grilled hamburgers</u>.
> They <u>made fruit salad</u>.
> The parents <u>poured water for everyone</u>.
>
> The parents <u>grilled hamburgers</u>, <u>made fruit salad</u>, **and** <u>poured
> water for everyone</u>.

D *Rewrite the underlined sentences in this journal entry on the
lines below. Combine each group of underlined sentences into
one sentence by using a series.*

    I wasn't looking forward to the class trip to the park. Now I'm glad I went.
<u>The trip was fun. It was interesting. The trip was educational.</u>

    I liked the nature walk best. <u>Along the way, I saw a red-tailed hawk. I saw
a Baltimore oriole. I saw a scarlet tanager.</u> I was also surprised by how many
different trees grow in the park. <u>Chestnut trees grow in the park. Walnut trees
grow there. Pecan trees grow in the park, too.</u>

    Back at the picnic tables, we had some more fun. Everyone gathered around
Ms. Grady, our teacher. <u>Ms. Grady handed out songbooks. She played the guitar.
She led a sing-along.</u> What a great way to end the day!

_____

_____

_____

_____

Lesson 47: **More Commas**

LEARN

Here are some more uses for commas.

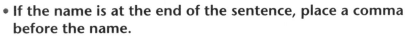

- Use a comma to set off an introductory word such as *yes*, *no*, or *well* from the rest of a sentence.

    Yes, I have some silly riddles to tell.
    No, not everyone likes them.
    Well, I think they're funny.

- Use a comma or commas to set off the name of a person being spoken to.

    - **If the name is at the beginning of the sentence, place a comma after the name.**
        Todd, what gets wet the more you dry?

    - **If the name is at the end of the sentence, place a comma before the name.**
        I don't know, **Ellen.**

    - **If the name is in the middle of the sentence, place commas before and after the name.**
        The answer, **Todd,** is a bath towel!

PRACTICE

A *Read each sentence. Write **introductory word** or **name of person spoken to** in order to tell what words are set off by the comma or commas.*

1. Michelle, do you know what gets bigger the more you take away from it? _____

2. No, I can't imagine what it could be. _____

3. The answer, Michelle, is a hole in the ground. _____

4. What crosses the country without moving, Tino? _____

5. Jodi, is this another silly riddle? _____

6. Yes, and the answer is a superhighway. _____

7. Avi, what breaks whenever you say it? _____

8. Hmm, I have no idea. _____

9. I think, Brenda, that the answer is "silence." _____

10. That is the correct answer, Tom! _____

B *In each sentence, add commas where they are needed. The first one is done for you.*

1. Do you know a place Bob where you can always find happiness?

2. Well let me think about that.

3. Ray is the answer "the dictionary"?

4. Yes you got it!

5. What coat is always wet when you put it on Nancy?

6. Hmm I think it's a coat of paint.

7. What is lighter than a feather Sandy but harder to hold?

8. Hmm could it be "a thought"?

9. No the answer is "your breath"!

10. Okay I have one for you.

11. Pam what's the difference between the North Pole and the South Pole?

12. It's all the difference in the world Ben!

13. You've heard Terri that two's company and three's a crowd.

14. Well do you know what four and five are?

15. Yes I know that four and five are nine!

C Leanne left out nine commas in the script that she wrote for the class comedy show. Find the mistakes, and use the proofreading marks in the box to correct the errors.

Remember

Use a comma after introductory words such as *yes* and *no*. Also, use a comma to set off the name of a person being spoken to.

Leanne	Akira, I hear things are looking up for your mom at work.
Akira	Yes, that's true. She just got a job as an astronomer.
Jamie	Hmm I thought she was a weather forecaster on TV Akira.
Akira	No not anymore Jamie. The weather here never agreed with her!
Jamie	Guys, my poor dad finds things really dull at his job.
Leanne	What kind of work does he do Jamie?
Jamie	Oh, he's a knife sharpener.
Leanne	My dad is a jeweler. He sells watches all day.
Akira	That's funny Leanne. My uncle watches cells all day. He works in a biology laboratory.
Jamie	I hear, Akira that you want to be a pilot someday.
Akira	Yes it's the type of job in which you can go really far! What about you, Jamie?
Jamie	Well I'm thinking about becoming a roofer. That way, I can go straight to the top!

Proofreading Marks

∧	Add
⊙	Period
ℒ	Take out
≡	Capital letter
/	Small letter

Did you add nine missing commas?

WRITE

D On the lines below, write your own funny script that shows a conversation between you and one or two friends. You can use jokes you know or a funny conversation you have heard for ideas. In your script, use introductory words and the names of people being spoken to. Use the script on page 214 as a model.

1. _____ _____

_____

_____

2. _____ _____

_____

_____

3. _____ _____

_____

_____

4. _____ _____

_____

_____

5. _____ _____

_____

_____

Proofreading Checklist ✓

❏ Did you use commas after introductory words such as **yes**, **no**, and **well**?

❏ Did you use commas to set off the names of people being spoken to?

Lesson 48: **Parts of a Letter**

LEARN

■ A **friendly letter** is written to someone you know well. In a friendly letter, the **greeting** and **closing** begin with a capital letter and end with a comma. Commas are also used in the **heading** to separate the city and state and to separate the day and year.

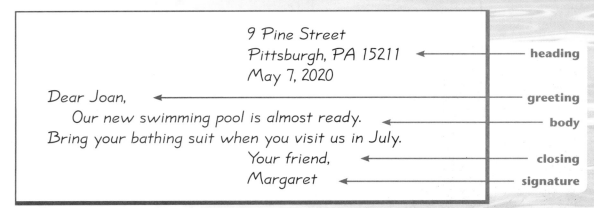

9 Pine Street
Pittsburgh, PA 15211 — heading
May 7, 2020

Dear Joan, — greeting
   Our new swimming pool is almost ready. — body
Bring your bathing suit when you visit us in July.
       Your friend, — closing
       Margaret — signature

■ A **business letter** is usually written to someone you don't know. In a business letter, include an **inside address** that gives the name and address of the person you are writing to. Use a **colon (:)** after the **greeting**. You will also need to sign and print your name.

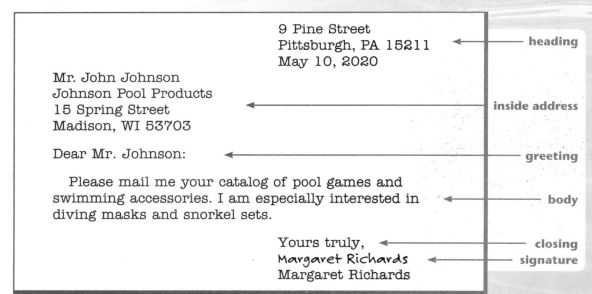

9 Pine Street
Pittsburgh, PA 15211 — heading
May 10, 2020

Mr. John Johnson
Johnson Pool Products
15 Spring Street — inside address
Madison, WI 53703

Dear Mr. Johnson: — greeting

   Please mail me your catalog of pool games and
swimming accessories. I am especially interested in — body
diving masks and snorkel sets.

       Yours truly, — closing
       Margaret Richards — signature
       Margaret Richards

PRACTICE

A *Write each letter part correctly.*

1. June, 17 2020 _____

2. Akron OH, 44319 _____

3. dear kenny _____

4. your Friend _____

5. dear Ms. Cahill _____

6. 21 fox lane _____

B *Complete the letter with the missing letter part.*
Write the letter part correctly.

> Gillette NJ 07933   184 ridge Road
> your friend   dear margaret

_____

_____

June 15, 2020

_____

I'm sorry to hear about the leak in your
new pool. I hope the pool company can fix it
soon. I know the whole family is looking
forward to using it this summer.

I can't wait to see you in July. We have so
much to catch up on.

_____

Joan

C *Margaret wrote this letter. In all, she made six mistakes in the use of capitalization and punctuation. Use the proofreading marks in the box to correct the errors.*

Proofreading Marks

∧	Add
⊙	Period
ℓ	Take out
≡	Capital letter
/	Small letter

9 Pine Street
Pittsburgh, pa 15211
June 28 2020

Ms. Tonya Ruiz
Community Park Recreation Center
111 Kensington Avenue
Pittsburgh PA 15211

Dear Ms. Ruiz

I heard that you will be offering swimming lessons for children under the age of 12 this summer. I am very interested in your swimming program. Please send me a schedule for these lessons.

sincerely Yours,
Margaret Richards
Margaret Richards

 Did you correct six mistakes in capitalization and punctuation?

Write
Your
Own

WRITE

D Write a friendly letter or a business letter. If you write a friendly letter, tell a friend or relative what you like most about school this year. If you write a business letter, make a suggestion to the principal of your school for a program or activity that your school might offer.

_____

_____

_____

_____

_____

_____

_____

_____

_____

_____

_____

_____

_____

_____

_____

_____

Proofreading Checklist ✔

❑ *Did you use commas and capital letters correctly in your letter?*
❑ *Did you use a comma after the greeting if you wrote a friendly letter?*
❑ *Did you use a colon after the greeting if you wrote a business letter?*

Lesson 49: **Quotations**

LEARN

■ A **quotation** is a speaker's or writer's exact words.
Follow these rules when writing quotations.

- Use quotation marks in *dialogue* or to set off a speaker's
  or writer's exact words. Always capitalize the first word
  of a quotation.

  Nancy said, "**L**ittle inventions make life easier."

- When a quotation comes at the end of a sentence, use a
  comma before the quotation to separate it from the words
  that name the speaker or writer. Put the end mark inside
  the quotation marks.

  Cy exclaimed**,** "How clever some inventors are**!**"

- When a quotation that is a statement or command comes
  at the beginning of a sentence, put a comma inside the
  closing quotation marks.

  "Harvey Kennedy invented shoelaces**,**" Nancy said.
  "Try living without them**,**" she added.

- If the quotation is a question or an exclamation, put the
  question mark or the exclamation mark inside the closing
  quotation marks.

  "Who invented the toothpaste tube**?**" Liam asked.
  "What a great invention that was**!**" I exclaimed.

■ Do not use quotation marks when you do not use a speaker's
or writer's exact words.

  Nancy said, "Let's look up the inventor's name."
  Nancy said that we should look up the inventor's name.

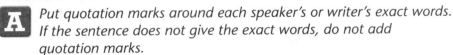

PRACTICE

A *Put quotation marks around each speaker's or writer's exact words.
If the sentence does not give the exact words, do not add
quotation marks.*

1. Terry claimed that the best inventions are very simple.

2. Liam said, Look at this picture of Benjamin Franklin.

3. He invented the lightning rod! Liam shouted.

4. How did he get the idea for it? Amy asked.

5. Liam said that Franklin wanted to protect buildings from lightning.

6. Mei said, Here's a picture of the first paper clip.

7. I asked, When was it invented?

8. It was invented in 1899 in Norway, Mei replied.

9. Nancy added that paper clips, tape, and ballpoint pens were all great inventions.

10. Where would we be without them? she asked.

B *Rewrite each sentence that is incorrectly written. Use quotation marks, capital letters, and punctuation marks correctly. If a sentence is correct as is, write **correct**.*

1. The traffic light was invented in 1923 Liam said. _____

_____

2. Who invented it asked Mei. _____

_____

3. Liam replied that the inventor was Garrett Morgan. _____

_____

4. Nancy said here's an 1883 picture of the first zipper. _____

_____

5. Terry asked how did it get its name? _____

_____

6. Nancy explained that the invention made a *z-z-zip* sound. _____

_____

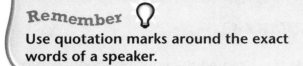

Remember
Use quotation marks around the exact words of a speaker.

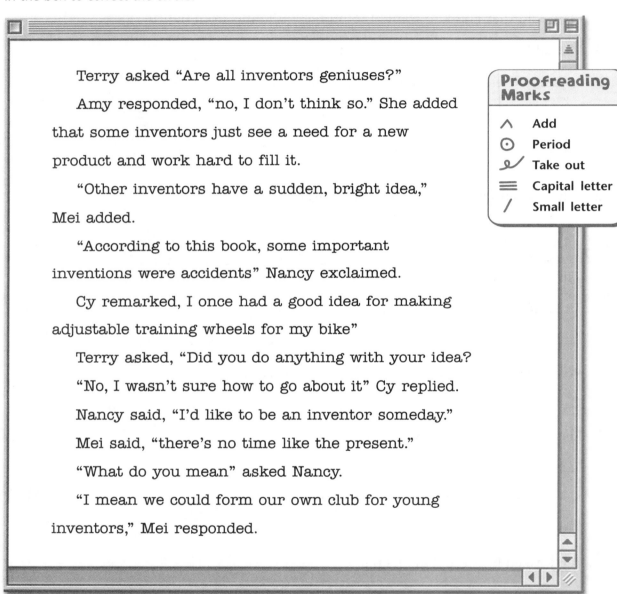

Terry asked "Are all inventors geniuses?"

Amy responded, "no, I don't think so." She added that some inventors just see a need for a new product and work hard to fill it.

"Other inventors have a sudden, bright idea," Mei added.

"According to this book, some important inventions were accidents" Nancy exclaimed.

Cy remarked, I once had a good idea for making adjustable training wheels for my bike"

Terry asked, "Did you do anything with your idea?

"No, I wasn't sure how to go about it" Cy replied.

Nancy said, "I'd like to be an inventor someday."

Mei said, "there's no time like the present."

"What do you mean" asked Nancy.

"I mean we could form our own club for young inventors," Mei responded.

Proofreading Marks

∧	Add
⊙	Period
ℓ⁄	Take out
≡	Capital letter
/	Small letter

Did you correct nine mistakes in punctuation and capitalization?

Write Your Own

WRITE

D *Imagine you are one of the students in the conversations below. Join each conversation by asking a question, making a statement, giving a command, or uttering an exclamation. Use quotation marks to set off your words.*

Conversation 1

"I have a great idea for an invention," Terry said.

"It's an electric sweater," she added.

"How would it work?" asked Cy.

"A battery would warm up the wires in the sleeves," Terry replied.

"I don't think that's very practical!" Liam exclaimed.

_____

_____

_____

Conversation 2

"Inventors need to patent their inventions," said Mr. Rossi, a local inventor.

"What's a patent?" Liam asked.

"It protects an inventor's ideas," Mei explained.

"It also makes it possible for an inventor to earn money from an invention," Mr. Rossi added.

_____

_____

_____

Proofreading Checklist ✓

❏ *Did you set off your words with quotation marks?*
❏ *Did you use capital letters, commas, quotation marks, and end marks correctly?*

Lesson 50: **Words Often Misspelled**

LEARN

■ **Homophones** are words that sound the same but have different spellings and meanings. Some homophones are possessive pronouns, such as *their*, and others are contractions, such as *they're*. Think about the meaning of the word to help you choose the correct spelling.

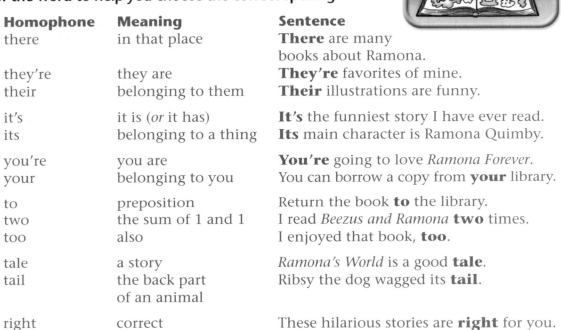

Homophone	Meaning	Sentence
there	in that place	**There** are many books about Ramona.
they're	they are	**They're** favorites of mine.
their	belonging to them	**Their** illustrations are funny.
it's	it is (*or* it has)	**It's** the funniest story I have ever read.
its	belonging to a thing	**Its** main character is Ramona Quimby.
you're	you are	**You're** going to love *Ramona Forever.*
your	belonging to you	You can borrow a copy from **your** library.
to	preposition	Return the book **to** the library.
two	the sum of 1 and 1	I read *Beezus and Ramona* **two** times.
too	also	I enjoyed that book, **too**.
tale	a story	*Ramona's World* is a good **tale**.
tail	the back part of an animal	Ribsy the dog wagged its **tail**.
right	correct	These hilarious stories are **right** for you.
write	create a story	The author can **write** a good tale.

■ When unsure which spelling is correct, use a dictionary.

PRACTICE

A *Write the meaning of each homophone. Then write* **contraction** *if the homophone is a contraction. Write* **possessive pronoun** *if it is a possessive pronoun. If it is neither, write* **neither**. *The first one is done for you.*

1. their   <u>belonging to them</u>   <u>possessive pronoun</u>

2. they're   _____   _____

3. there   _____   _____

4. its _____   _____

5. right _____   _____

6. you're _____   _____

7. tail _____   _____

8. too _____   _____

B *Write the homophone in parentheses that correctly completes each sentence.*

1. Will you bring your copy of *Ramona's World* _____ school? (to, too)

2. _____ a popular book among young readers. (Its, It's)

3. Beverly Cleary is _____ author. (its, it's)

4. She grew up in Oregon, and her stories are set _____. (their, there)

5. I have read _____ of her books. (two, too)

6. You are _____ about her books. (right, write)

7. It may even make you want to _____ your own Ramona adventure. (right, write)

8. You might enjoy a book called *Henry and Ribsy*, _____. (to, too)

9. It is a _____ about Henry Huggins and his dog Ribsy. (tale, tail)

10. _____ neighborhood was once a quiet place. (There, Their)

11. _____ up to Henry and Ribsy to change that! (Its, It's)

12. _____ sure to love Beverly Cleary's books. (Your, You're)

C *Maria wrote this book report. She made six mistakes when using homophones. Use the proofreading marks in the box to correct the errors.*

Remember 💡
When using homophones, pay attention to the way they are used. For example, *they're*, *it's*, and *you're* are contractions, while *their*, *its*, and *your* are possessive pronouns that show ownership.

<u>Ramona's World</u> by Beverly Cleary is a very funny book. Its a story about the kind of everyday events all of us can recognize. There told in such a humorous way that they cause everyone too laugh.

When the book begins, it is the first day of school. Ramona is looking forward to an exciting year, but there are a few problems, two. Ramona's teacher likes her first essay, but it's filled with misspelled words. When the teacher begins to right the mistakes on the board, Ramona is horrified.

On the bright side, Ramona and Daisy Kidd become friends. One day, they're playing in an upstairs crawl space. Its floor is only a layer of plaster, and Ramona's legs break through the attic. Is she hurt? Are you curious? Read the book. Your sure to enjoy it.

Proofreading Marks

∧	Add
⊙	Period
ℯ	Take out
≡	Capital letter
/	Small letter

Did you correct six spelling mistakes?

Write
Your
Own

WRITE

D Write a short book report about a book you've enjoyed recently.
Be sure to give the title and author of the book. Then give your
opinion about the book. Tell why you think your classmates might enjoy
the book, too. Use some of the homophones below in your report.

it's	its	you're	your	they're
there	their	to	too	two
right	write	tail	tale	

_____

_____

_____

_____

_____

_____

_____

_____

_____

_____

Proofreading Checklist ✔

❏ *Did you use some of the homophones in your report?*
❏ *Did you spell each homophone correctly?*

Lesson 51: **Words Often Confused**

LEARN

■ When two words sound alike or are similar in spelling, the two words can be confused. For example, the word *advice* is often confused with the word *advise*. To avoid confusion, learn the meaning and spelling of each word. *Advice* is helpful information you give to someone. When you *advise* someone, you give him or her a helpful suggestion.

> Our teacher gave us **advice** on ways to prepare for test day.
> He said, "I **advise** you all to stop studying tonight and to sleep well."

■ If you are unsure of which word to use, you can use a dictionary.

PRACTICE

A *Match each word in Column A to its meaning in Column B. Write the letter of the correct meaning on the line. If you are unsure of the meaning, check a dictionary.*

A	*B*
_____ **1.** desert	**a.** the star that Earth revolves around
_____ **2.** proof	**b.** more distant
_____ **3.** all ready	**c.** to show that something is true
_____ **4.** further	**d.** dry, sandy land
_____ **5.** sun	**e.** a male child
_____ **6.** by	**f.** in addition to something
_____ **7.** prove	**g.** by this time
_____ **8.** dessert	**h.** a sweet food served at the end of a meal
_____ **9.** farther	**i.** preposition that tells who/what did the action
_____ **10.** already	**j.** completely ready

_____ **11.** buy   **k.** to get something by paying for it with money

_____ **12.** son   **l.** evidence

B   *Write the word in parentheses that correctly completes each sentence.*

1. Today, we had to write our favorite

_____ recipes.
(desert, dessert)

2. My favorite recipe for lemon cookies was

given to me _____ my
great grandmother. (buy, by)

3. The first step in my recipe is to

_____ all the ingredients.
(buy, by)

4. When mixing the batter, I would _____ everyone
to use a wooden spoon. (advice, advise)

5. If you want to go a step _____, try making a
lemon frosting. (farther, further)

6. Today, a guest chef and his _____ came to our school. (sun, son)

7. They gave our class _____ on how to bake bread. (advice, advise)

8. They said that the _____ of a good baker is "in
the pudding." (prove, proof)

9. It was _____ time for lunch when the chef took fresh baked
bread out of the oven. (all ready, already)

10. I took a loaf of bread home to _____ to my family
that I am now a real baker! (proof, prove)

C Raj wrote this journal entry about his art class. He made six mistakes when writing words that are often confused. Find the mistakes, and use the proofreading marks in the box to correct the errors.

Remember 💡
Use the word with the intended meaning. Spell the word carefully.

Today in art class, our teacher, Ms. Nova, described a scene and asked us to paint it. Before we started, we each got a piece of paper and some paints. When we were already, she started to read the description.

Ms. Nova talked about cactuses, sand, and tumbleweed. That's when I knew she was describing a dessert. I quickly picked up my pencil and started drawing. Then I used watercolors to fill in my drawing. I had a few green cactus plants in front. Further away were sandy, brown hills. Beyond this, I could think of nothing farther to draw! That's when I asked Ms. Nova for advise. She told me to close my eyes and imagine the picture again. When I opened my eyes, I knew just what to add. I drew a bright, orange son, a scaly iguana, and a flying eagle that soared through the air. I was so happy with my colorful desert scene that I couldn't wait to take it home!

Proofreading Marks

∧	Add
⊙	Period
ℰ	Take out
≡	Capital letter
/	Small letter

Did you use the correct meaning of six words that are often confused?

WRITE

D *Write sentences about how to make or do something.*
Use the word in parentheses in each sentence.

1. (already) _____

_____

2. (advice) _____

_____

3. (sun) _____

_____

4. (proof) _____

_____

5. (buy) _____

_____

6. (further) _____

_____

7. (all ready) _____

_____

8. (prove) _____

_____

Proofreading Checklist ☑

❏ *Did you use each word in parentheses correctly?*

Writing Sentences Correctly (pp. 192–195) *Write each sentence correctly. Write each run-on sentence as two sentences.*

1. what sorts of things do you collect

_____

2. we have many cards we trade them sometimes

_____

3. what a great collection you have

_____

Capitalizing Proper Nouns (pp. 196–199) *Read each sentence. Write each proper noun correctly.*

4. My aunt lives near golden gate park.   _____

5. We visited her on the fourth of july.   _____

6. I gave aunt betty a small figurine of a cat.   _____

Abbreviations (pp. 200–203) *Write each name or abbreviation correctly.*

7. dr Vivian Hayes   _____

8. thurs   _____

9. mr Donald a Banks   _____

10. p o Box 124   _____

Titles (pp. 204–207) *Write each title correctly.*

11. the mouse and the motorcycle (book)   _____

12. a day at the beach (poem)   _____

13. sports illustrated for kids (magazine)   _____

Commas (pp. 208–215) *In each sentence, add commas where they are needed.*

14. My mother father and brother all collect things.

15. Mom do you collect old maps?

Parts of a Letter (pp. 216–219) *Write each letter part correctly.*

16. dear Charlie

17. sincerely yours

18. Baltimore MD 21202

19. dear Mayor Hanks

Quotations (pp. 220–223) *Add commas and quotation marks where necessary to show each speaker's words.*

20. Claire said Everyone in my family collects something except me.

21. Mimi asked How many miniature horses do you have on your dresser?

22. I guess I have a collection after all! Claire laughed.

Words Often Misspelled (pp. 224–227) *Underline the homophone in parentheses that correctly completes each sentence.*

23. (Their, There) will be a doll auction this weekend.

24. Mia's cousin likes to attend doll auctions, (to, too).

25. (Your, You're) favorite hobby is collecting art.

26. (Its, It's) a family tradition to go to auctions every spring break.

Words Often Confused (pp. 228–231) *Underline the word in parentheses that correctly completes each sentence.*

27. A furniture collector can (prove, proof) that Fran's chair is worth a lot of money.

28. At the auction, her chair is (farther, further) down the aisle.

29. To get (advise, advice) on collecting comics, Mike spoke to an expert.

30. The annual auction was (already, all ready) closed to the public.

TIP

Remember, you can find out more about capitalization, punctuation, and spelling on pages 192–231.

PROOFREADING PRACTICE

Read the text below. There are 15 mistakes in the use of capitalization, punctuation, and spelling. Use the proofreading marks in the box to correct them.

173 Plum blvd.

Chicago, IL 60640

Oct. 4, 2020

Proofreading Marks	
∧	Add
⊙	Period
ℒ	Take out
≡	Capital letter
/	Small letter

Dear Ms. lopez,

I'm writing to invite you to my school's talent show on Friday, Nov. 15 it'll be a grate show. I'm going to wow the crowd by reciting "Jabberwocky. It was written by Lewis Carroll, who wrote Alice's adventures in Wonderland.

Do you remember my friend Steve. He's going to juggle an apple, a pear and an orange. my friend Chen and his dog have an amazing trick. His dog, apollo, can balance a ball on his nose while wagging his tale. There's also a bake sale with great deserts!

I think you'll enjoy this show. The school's address is 419 Plum Blvd. in chicago. It's buy the park. Hope to see you then!

Sincerely,

Jesse

WRITE ABOUT IT

Write a letter telling a friend about an act in a school talent show. Use details from the text on page 234. Include names and abbreviations in your letter. Use the Writing Process Handbook on pages 236–251 to help you plan. When you are finished writing your draft, then proofread your work.

_____

_____

_____

_____

_____

_____

_____

Check It Out! ☑

Did you . . .
- ❑ write a letter telling a friend about an act in a school talent show?
- ❑ use details from the text on page 234?
- ❑ include a heading, greeting, and closing?
- ❑ include names and abbreviations?
- ❑ revise and edit your writing to show what you learned about sentence structure, abbreviations, and commas?
- ❑ proofread for correct spelling, capitalization, and punctuation?

TALK ABOUT IT

Discuss: _What is your talent? What would you do in a school talent show? Describe a skill you would like to learn. Talk about why you would like to learn this skill._

WRITING PROCESS HANDBOOK

The first six units of *Grammar Workshop* have taught you grammar, usage, spelling, mechanics, and punctuation. These skills are very important when you start to create your own writing.

Whether you are writing an informational text or a story, you will use the guidelines of good writing, but you will also need to know the Writing Process. These are the steps that will help you develop pieces of writing.

The Writing Process Handbook will teach you about the stages of the Writing Process. Once you know them, you can apply them to any type of writing you do.

A good writer knows that there are different stages in creating a piece of writing. In this handbook, you will learn how to work through each one. Writers follow these stages no matter what type or genre of writing they are creating.

The Writing Process:

- planning
- drafting
- revising
- editing
- producing, publishing, and presenting

These stages usually follow a specific order, but writers may need to go back to earlier stages as they develop their work. For example, in drafting a story, you may decide to gather more details, or in revising an informational text, you may need to draft a completely new paragraph. Be open to being flexible in your writing process if it will help you make a better final product.

Planning

LEARN

If you were building a house, you wouldn't start with a stack of wood and a saw. You'd have to do a lot of planning before you ever picked up a tool. Writing is the same way. **Planning** is the first stage of the Writing Process, and if you do it well, your planning choices will make it easier to get to your final draft.

Follow these steps when you are planning your writing:

- Brainstorm a list of possible topics for writing and then choose one.
- Choose the type of writing or genre that you are going to write.
- Decide on your purpose for writing and identify your audience.
- Collect and organize details and evidence to include in your writing.

Ⓐ Choosing a Topic

In school you may be given a **topic** or a writing prompt before you begin the Writing Process. To help you choose your own topic for your writing, spend time getting ideas flowing. You can use strategies like these to get started.

1. **Freewrite:** Start with a word, a general topic, or a photograph to spark ideas. For five minutes, write down every thought you have about it. When you are done, review your work and choose a topic.

2. **Web:** Use one or two words to lead you to more specific ideas. Instead of writing full sentences, make a web. Put a general idea in the center, and then write the ideas it sparks in circles that come off the center. Then, review your web and choose a topic.

When he was asked to write about an important event in his life, Ben made this web to begin to list his ideas. From this list, he chose the topic "When I stood up to a bully at school."

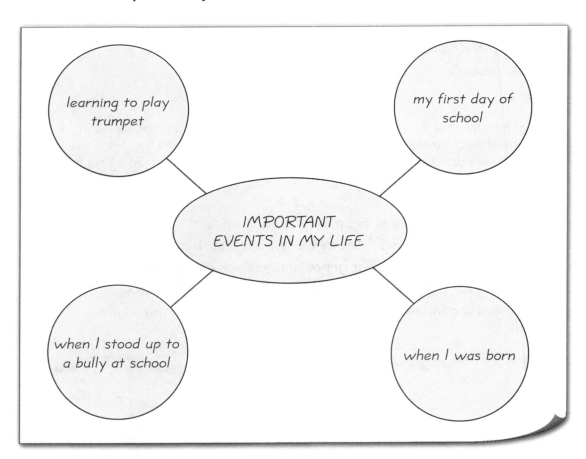

On a sheet of paper, either freewrite or make a web to choose your topic.

Make sure:

• you feel strongly about your topic.

• there is enough information available about the topic.

• the topic is appropriate for the assignment.

When you are done, complete this sentence:

The topic I will write about is _____.

B Choosing a Genre

In school you may be assigned a specific type or **genre** of writing. However, if you are writing for your own reasons, you may need to think about the type of writing you want to do. Here is a list of genres that you might consider before you write:

Genre	Definition
Informative/ Explanatory	Writing that gives readers information about a specific topic to help them understand it
Persuasive	Writing that tells your opinion about a specific topic and tries to convince readers to have that same opinion
Narrative	Writing that tells a story, real or imaginary
Response to Literature	Writing that shares an opinion or states an idea about the theme, plot, character, main idea, message, or quality of another text

Complete this sentence to choose your genre:

The genre I am writing is _____.

C Choosing a Purpose

The **purpose**, or reason, you are writing plays an important part in the types of details you include. Here are some common purposes for writing:

- To entertain: Share an experience or an idea with your readers.
- To describe: Detail an event, person, place, or thing that has meaning to you.
- To explain: Show your readers how to do something or why something/someone is important to you.
- To persuade: Convince your readers through argument to agree with your idea or to act in a certain way.

Complete these sentences to help you choose your purpose.

The main thing I want my readers to learn is _____.

I want to share this topic with other people because _____.

Now complete this sentence:

My purpose is _____.

D Choosing an Audience

If you are building a house, you will speak differently to the people who will live in it than you might to the workers who are building it. You share different information. When you write, think about your **audience**, the specific readers you want to read your work.

Ask yourself who your readers will be and what information they may already know about your topic.

My audience is _____.

Complete a chart like the one below to help you focus on your audience.

What They Already Know About the Topic	What They Need to Know About the Topic
• • • • •	• • • • •

E Collecting Details and Evidence

The last step in planning is to gather information about your topic and organize it in a way that makes sense. Just like gathering the materials you need before beginning to build the house, having details and evidence ready before you write makes the drafting stage easier. Here's how to **collect details and evidence**:

1. Review your topic, purpose, and audience.

2. Go to your local or school library, or use online resources, to read about your topic. You can also talk to people who know more about your topic than you do.

3. Jot down a list of specific details you want to include or complete a graphic organizer. You may want to group details into categories to help you plan.

To write about the important event in his life, Ben put the details of his narrative in order by using a graphic organizer:

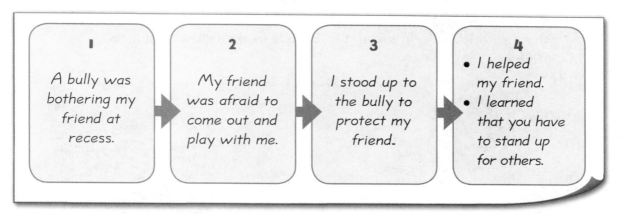

1	**2**	**3**	**4**
A bully was bothering my friend at recess.	My friend was afraid to come out and play with me.	I stood up to the bully to protect my friend.	• I helped my friend. • I learned that you have to stand up for others.

On a sheet of paper, jot down a list of details and evidence, or complete a graphic organizer to collect ideas about your topic.

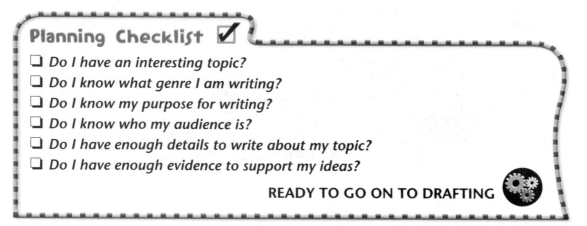

Planning Checklist ☑

❑ *Do I have an interesting topic?*
❑ *Do I know what genre I am writing?*
❑ *Do I know my purpose for writing?*
❑ *Do I know who my audience is?*
❑ *Do I have enough details to write about my topic?*
❑ *Do I have enough evidence to support my ideas?*

READY TO GO ON TO DRAFTING

Drafting

LEARN

If you are building a house, once you've made your plan, you have to build the structure. Likewise, once you have planned your writing, you have to get your ideas down in a draft. **Drafting** is the next stage in the Writing Process. In later stages, you will polish your work to make it better.

Take the following steps when you are drafting:

- **Plan the structure of your draft.** Organize your writing into a structure that makes sense.
  - For informative, explanatory, and opinion writing, use an introduction, body paragraphs, and a conclusion.
  - For narratives create a beginning, middle, and end.
- **Write your draft.** Include as much detail and information as you need to share your ideas. Don't forget to include evidence that supports your ideas.

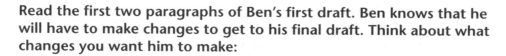

A Planning a Draft

*When **planning a draft**, review your plan to be sure you have a structure that works. Then think about what you want to include in each part of your draft.*

Read the first two paragraphs of Ben's first draft. Ben knows that he will have to make changes to get to his final draft. Think about what changes you want him to make:

An important event in my life was when I stood up to a bully. I also learned to play the trumpet and it was fun. I wanted to play outside with my friend. He would not play with me. But I kept asking. He finally said yes. "Stop! You can't speak to him like that!" I could not believe I said that but I did! I had seen Joe be mean to other kids before. But this time was different. I had to say something.

It all started about a month ago. At recess I saw my best friend james kept choosing to stay in the classroom and help our teacher instead of coming out to play.

What idea will you want to share in your first paragraph to grab your reader's attention?

The idea I want to share is _____.

B Writing a Draft

On a separate sheet of paper, write a complete draft based on your notes and plan.

Here are some additional suggestions for the drafting stage:

- Just start writing. Don't stop to wonder if you should include an idea. Include it. You can always remove it later.

- Use the words you want, even if you are not sure how to spell them.

- Be ready to change your plan as you write. You may find the plan doesn't work the way you thought it would.

- Write clearly. Leave space between lines so that you have room to revise and edit later. If you are word processing, use double space.

- If you are writing about a piece of literature, include details and evidence from the text to support your ideas.

Drafting Checklist ✓

- ❏ *Did I stay focused on my topic?*
- ❏ *Did I support my main point?*
- ❏ *Have I selected the important details and evidence in my planning notes?*
- ❏ *Did drafting spark some additional ideas?*
- ❏ *Do I need to go back to planning to gather more details?*

READY TO GO ON TO REVISING

Revising

LEARN

If you are building a house, you may find that something doesn't quite work where it is. You must think about ways to improve it, and writing is no different. Now that you have finished your first draft, the next stage is to improve it. During the **revising** stage of the Writing Process, reread your draft and decide what works and what doesn't. When you revise, you focus on the ideas of your writing. You can fix spelling and mechanics later.

Steps for revising:

- Start with structure. Be sure that the order of your paragraphs make sense.
- Review every paragraph and every sentence to be sure the ideas flow.
- Add or remove details and evidence to make your writing clearer.
- Improve your word choice by replacing weak words with stronger ones.
- Ask someone else to read your work and give you suggestions for improving it.
- Add transitional words and phrases to make your writing flow better.

Here is the same part of Ben's draft with his notes for revising:

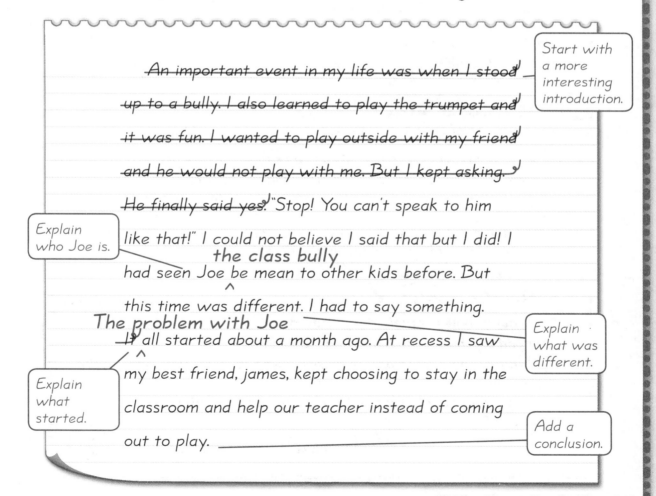

A Doing a Peer Review

*Trade drafts with a partner. Use these guidelines to do a **peer review**.*

Review your partner's work:

- Always start with a positive comment. Tell your partner what you liked best about the draft.
- Mark places in the draft that are confusing or where you have questions. This will show your partner areas that need more detail and evidence or more attention.
- Give specific feedback so your partner knows what to do next.

Get your partner's feedback:

- If there is something that you want help with, ask your partner for advice.
- After your partner is finished, have a conversation about your draft.
- Review the notes on your draft. It is your work, so you decide which changes you want to make.

> **TIP** 💡
> Be positive! Remember, your goal is to help your partner. Offer suggestions in a positive and specific way. Instead of saying, "This part doesn't sound good," you can say, "This part doesn't flow well. You may want to add a transition here."

B Revising a Draft

Now it is time to revise your draft on your own.

Review your draft. Follow these steps to review your draft.

- Use the Steps for Revising on page 245 and mark changes on your draft.
- Review your partner's suggestions and decide which of the suggestions you will use.
- Write a clean draft of your writing with all of the changes from your revision. This will make it easier for you to edit in the next step.

Revising Checklist ✔

- ❑ *Did I change how I organized my ideas to make my writing clearer?*
- ❑ *Did I add or remove details and evidence to improve my writing?*
- ❑ *Did I change any of my words to make my writing more interesting, precise, or powerful?*
- ❑ *Did I add transitional words and phrases to make my writing flow better?*

READY TO GO ON TO EDITING ⚙

Editing

LEARN

If you are building a house, once the improvements are complete, you have to make sure that everything in the house works perfectly. Similarly, when you write you have to make sure your work is correct. Now that you have a clean, revised draft of your writing, it is time to move on to the next stage in the Writing Process, **editing**. At this stage you correct any errors in grammar, usage, spelling, mechanics, and punctuation.

Take the following steps when you are editing:

- Carefully read your writing more than once. Each time you read it, focus on one thing. If you try to check too many things at one time, it is much easier to miss errors. Make sure your work is correct according to the rules of good writing.

- Read your paper out loud slowly, sentence by sentence. Hearing your writing this way may help you catch mistakes you may have missed.

Use questions like these to help you edit your writing:

Editing Questions	■ Yes	■ No
Grammar		
Do the subject and verb of each sentence agree?		
Is the verb tense the same throughout the writing?		
Do pronouns match the nouns they replace?		
Mechanics		
Does every sentence start with a capital letter and end with the right punctuation mark?		
Are punctuation marks, such as commas and quotations, used correctly?		
Are all paragraphs indented?		
Usage		
Are the words the correct ones, especially when using commonly confused words such as *to*, *two*, and *too*?		
Is every word spelled correctly?		

Use proofreading marks.

- When you edit your writing, use proofreading marks to indicate the mistakes on your paper.
- Write your corrections neatly so it will be easy for you to read them when you write your final draft.

Here are some common proofreading marks:

Proofreading Marks

∧	Add	≡	Capital letter
⊙	Period	/	Small letter
ℰ	Take out	¶	Paragraph

Here is the proofread version of Ben's draft:

"Stop! You can't speak to him like that!" I could not believe I said that but I did! I had seen Joe the class bully be mean to other kids before⊙ ∧ But this time was different. He was doing it to my best friend so I had to say something. The shocking part is he was so surprised I stood up to him that he stopped. It is important to stand up for other people, because you can really make a difference.

¶ The problem with Joe ~~all~~ started about a month ago. At recess I saw my best friend, james, kept choosing to stay in the classroom and help our teacher instead of coming out to play. But now, James is no longer scared to play at recess.

A Checking Your Draft

When **checking your draft**, use a different color pencil or pen to edit your revised draft.

Follow these steps to edit your writing:

• Use the Editing Questions to review your writing.

• Use the proofreading marks to indicate your changes neatly.

• Create a clean copy of your writing.

Here is the final version of Ben's writing:

"Stop! You can't speak to him like that!" I could not believe I said that, but I did! I had seen Joe the class bully be mean to other kids before, but this time was different. He was doing it to my best friend so I had to say something. The shocking part is he was so surprised I stood up to him that he stopped. It is important to stand up for other people, because you can really make a difference.

The problem with Joe started about a month ago. At recess I saw my best friend, James, kept choosing to stay in the classroom and help our teacher instead of coming out to play. But now, James is no longer scared to play at recess.

Editing Checklist ✔

❏ Did I review my work to find and correct all errors in grammar, usage, and mechanics?

❏ Did I create a final, error-free copy?

❏ Is my final draft neat and easy to read?

READY TO GO ON TO PRODUCING, PUBLISHING, AND PRESENTING

Producing, Publishing, and Presenting

LEARN

If you are building a house, the last step you take is presenting it to the people who will live there. Likewise, the last stage in the Writing Process is **producing, publishing, and presenting**. During this stage, you share a final copy of your writing and present your ideas to your audience.

Follow these steps to produce, publish, and present your writing:

- Give your writing a title.
- Share your writing with others.
- Reflect on your writing to continue to improve your skills.

Be creative about the way you share your work with others. Try one of these ways to present your writing:

Presentation Type	Explanation	Examples
Oral Presentation	Speak to a group about your topic.	• Small-group presentation • Speech to the class • School assembly
Written Paper	Put your writing in print for a wider audience.	• Blog • School newspaper • Class newsletter
Multimedia Presentation	Add technology to help share your ideas.	• Class presentation with pictures and music • Slide show • Skit • Video

A Making a Presentation

*Once you have chosen how you want to share your writing, get all the materials you need and prepare your **presentation**.*

■ Rehearse your presentation. Practice reading your work a few times to make sure you'll feel comfortable in front of a group.

■ Present your work to the class, school, or small group.

■ Ask for comments and be ready to answer questions from your audience.

B Reflecting on Your Writing

After you finish a piece of writing, take some time to think about what you learned from the experience. Think about your work and then answer these questions:

1. What did you do well in this assignment?

_____

_____

2. What do you want to continue to work on in your next assignment?

_____

_____

Producing, Publishing, and Presenting Checklist ✓

❏ *Did my presentation go smoothly?*
❏ *What can I learn from my presentation that might help me the next time I share my writing?*

You have now completed the Writing Process Handbook. You can use the stages of the Writing Process whenever you write.

INDEX